CREATIVE
TV WRITING

TONY BICÂT

FOREWORD BY NIGEL STAFFORD-CLARK

CROWOOD

First published in 2007 by
The Crowood Press Ltd
Ramsbury, Marlborough
Wiltshire SN8 2HR

www.crowood.com

British Library Cataloguing-in-Publication Data
A catalogue record for this book is available from the British Library.

ISBN 978 1 86126 922 5

Typeset by S R Nova Pvt Ltd., Bangalore, India

Printed and bound in Spain by GraphyCems

Contents

FOREWORD

by Nigel Stafford-Clark

Television is celebrated as the writer's medium, yet the best-known books on scriptwriting are aimed at the big screen rather than the small one. That's always seemed odd to me. If you think about film, the names that come into your head are directors – Hitchcock, Scorsese, Spielberg, Huston. Try it with television and the names are those of writers – Steven Bochco, Alan Ball, Jimmy McGovern, Paul Abbott. Feature film writers get paid a lot in Hollywood, but with very few exceptions it's a dog's life. Most of their work is never produced, and on the rare occasions it is, they're often replaced after a couple of drafts by someone else, who's then replaced in their turn, until the original writer's vision has all but vanished. In television, the writer has a much better chance of creating a piece of work and seeing it safely through to an audience that, though increasingly fragmented, is still huge by the standards of any other performing art.

So why the bias towards feature film? I suppose it's because screenwriting lends itself to a series of more or less didactic rules – the 'follow this and you can't go wrong' school, which I've always deeply distrusted. Television is much more difficult to pin down. Drama, comedy, soap – each makes very particular demands on the writer. And they split into a dizzying array of subdivisions. Drama can mean a single film, or a serial which is one long story split into episodes, or a series which involves the same characters and setting but a different story each week. Except that it might also include a serial element. And the episodes can be anything from half an hour to two hours long. You can see why a book about writing for television might feel like a daunting prospect.

As a producer, I've always believed that it all comes down to the script. Without a strong script, you're making bricks without straw. In television, particularly, there is no great programme without a great script behind it. Whether it's Andrew Davies adapting *Pride and Prejudice*, Jimmy McGovern's *Cracker*, Ricky Gervais and Stephen Merchant with *The Office*, or Galton and Simpson with *Hancock*, it's all about the quality of the writing.

So I welcome this book because it fills a gap. But more than that, I welcome it because it approaches its subject with a refreshing lack of dogma. It noses out the common ground between different genres, but it also covers the special demands that each will make. It will help you avoid pitfalls, but won't limit your exploration of your own style and vision. Above all, it is full of glorious examples of television writing at its very best, which is not only immensely instructive, but also wonderfully heartening. As you sit poised above that blank sheet of paper, it's good to know that Steven Bochco must have been in exactly the same place just before he wrote the opening episode of *Hill Street Blues*.

Nigel Stafford-Clark has been producing film and television drama since the 1980s. He has won the Best Serial award from BAFTA three times in the last seven years and his television productions include Shoot To Kill, Warriors, The Way We Live Now *and* Bleak House.

DEDICATION

For David Rose and all my producers, who took the risk.

ACKNOWLEDGEMENTS

I would like to thank the following for information, useful discussion and other kinds of help – Peter Ansorge, Marc Berlin, Cleo Bicât, Nick Bicât, Hilary Briegel, Peter Buckman, Jenny Gaskin, David Hare, Alison Jackson, Robert Llcwellen, Laura Mackie, Tony Macnabb, Nigel McCreery, Bill Shapter, Frances Whitaker, Minette Walters, Michael Wearing and many other friends and students.

Preface

I grew up in a house without a television set, a member of the last generation to do so. I used to crawl through a hole in the hedge to watch TV at a neighbour's. It seemed then to be a window on an extraordinary world of variety, satire and, of course, drama. I fell in love with the medium and wanted to be part of it. I did some work experience at Granada TV in Manchester before going to university. After university, I worked in fringe theatre and made two films financed by The British Film Institute, also working for the BFI as a producer. A lot of rejected 'spec scripts' later, I began to write and direct original drama for TV.

I was lucky to fall into a period when there was a lot of original drama, by which I mean drama created specifically for the medium. It wasn't, although it has been portrayed as such, quite a golden age. There were many things wrong with British TV then; with today's eyes it would doubtless be regarded as institutionally sexist and racist. It was certainly dominated by an Oxbridge 'mafia' with a mindset that managed to be both vaguely liberal but also curiously restrictive, particularly as regards what TV drama ought to be.

However, at the BBC in Birmingham, David Rose ran a drama department that was outside the mainstream. He positively encouraged creative dissonance. With his department I wrote and directed TV films and, when he started the drama department at the new Channel Four, I moved with him. I continued to work in 'the cracks in the pavement' until, in the fall-out from the 1990 UK Broadcasting Act, and the Birtian reforms at the BBC, those cracks were filled in.

In the climate of the late nineties, writer/directors were regarded with intense suspicion and I found myself adapting novels and script-doctoring. I worked a lot with students using the new technology to teach and experiment with my own writing and directing. In the twenty-first century I came back to TV, thanks to the new digital channels. Finding myself, in my fourth decade in the medium, working for the youth channel BBC 3. I wrote the librettos for the multi-award winning live TV operas, *Flashmob The Opera* and *Brand New Flashmob*.

I have never lost my love for TV. Television's virtue and vice is that it must be embraced whole. Everything about the medium, its technological developments, its sometimes grotesque programmes and its extraordinary influence on our society, informs the way we write for it. It is the antithesis of the ivory tower. However, being aware of the medium does not mean that writers should be in awe of it. British TV drama, despite acres of executives and mountains of audience research, is still dominated by three strongly individualistic writers: Jimmy McGovern, Paul Abbot and Russell T. Davis, whose work would stand out in any context. Similarly, American TV is lent unparalleled kudos by David Chase, Aaron Sorkin and Alan Ball. However TV is delivered, and however much we post our home-made efforts on You Tube, there will always be room for strong writing.

This book is a personal book. It is by no means definitive and is about exactly what it says on the cover: Creative TV Writing. My intention, as with the workshops I do, is to help students and professionals to think about their work in a more creative way, to watch TV critically and in such a way that they can apply that critical analysis to their writing. There is now so much advice out there on script writing, so many theories of drama, that I have coined the word 'scripturgy' to describe it. Scripturgy is not in itself malevolent but there is altogether too much of it. It makes the heads of students reel and it also gives a language to unimaginative executives to bully writers; in Stephen Gagan's phrase, 'It allows accountants to talk about scripts'.

This is a short book. It won't tell you everything but it will tell you enough to get you started. If you are already writing, it may make you look in places you would not have thought of looking. If you are blocked, hopefully it may unblock you.

In 2002 Tony Macnabb and I co-wrote *Creative Screenwriting*, which dealt with writing for the movies. This book was the culmination of the many workshops we had run at the Short Course Unit at The National Film and TV School, and elsewhere in the UK and abroad. The feedback we have had since its publication has been good. We have had endorsements from both established screenwriters and novices. In some places *Creative Screenwriting* is being used as a textbook. I am greatly indebted in this book to Tony Macnabb, for constant encouragement, ideas and critiques, not to mention his excellent DVD library – none of which I could have done without.

1 INTRODUCTION

WHERE TO BEGIN?

When you consider the wealth and enormous variety of television drama world-wide, the maths are staggering. On the five UK TV terrestrial channels, there are over forty hours of episodic drama per week; then there are the repeats and the satellite channels. The famous Brazilian tele-novellas often run to hundreds of episodes per storyline. There are Chinese, Japanese, Indian and Scandinavian soaps and dubbed versions of our home-grown ones as well. No book could ever be exhaustive, so *Creative TV Writing* will not attempt the impossible. Instead I will be selective and analyse in depth only a few shows per chapter. Moreover, this analysis will generally deal with only one aspect of the chosen show, e.g. character, dialogue or structure.

The speed of technological development and the constant commercial pressures on the medium make it daily more and more unpredictable. Writers writing for TV must be very aware that they are writing for a market-driven, audience-chasing medium that is changing all the time.

TV can so easily degenerate into a meaningless white noise, just another part of the cacophony of twenty-first century life. To work successfully in it the writer must be able to tune this out and concentrate on specific detail. It is much better for the aspiring writer to thoroughly understand one particular technique than to attempt the impossible and grasp everything in one go.

WHAT DO THEY WANT?

Writers ask, 'What do producers want?', while producers ask, 'What do the audience want?' – the answer is always the same: a hit. The trouble is nobody knows what is going to be a hit. They know what the last hit was and for this reason TV writers are frequently asked to provide copycat shows. Moreover, particularly in UK TV, the format for this mysterious 'hit' changes. The edict will go out: 'We need more returnable series'; but by the time the writing community has worked up a fistful of cracking formats, the broadcasters will have decided that mini-series are what are needed now. Writers and their producers have to go back to the drawing board!

TV writers may write with their eyes on the stars but their feet will always be planted squarely in the market-place. He or she is, more than almost any other writer, a hack; but they can be a noble hack; and he or she, if successful, can be a very rich hack.

WRITING ABOUT WRITING FOR TV

If writing for TV is a constantly changing process, writing about writing for TV is even worse. What is perfectly sensible advice today, may not seem to be so sensible tomorrow and by next week may appear positively deranged. It is all too easy to become cynical about TV drama. The enormous volume of product required by the medium, the fact that much of it is written at great speed and that scripts are frequently rewritten at the whim of executives and schedulers bowing to the latest fashion, makes it a wonder that any of it is any good at all.

So the choice is both personal and partial. These are mostly ground-breaking shows but they are also shows I like and admire. I believe that if we coolly analyse them and try to see how they are written and constructed, we can establish certain principles of episodic storytelling. This study will give channel-markers to the aspiring TV writer and hopefully increase the number of hours of creative writing on TV.

HOW TO USE THIS BOOK

The path I take in examining the shows I will discuss, generally looks like this:

Step outline of episode
⇓
Analysis of that step outline
⇓
Commentary on that analysis
⇓
Some sound principles to apply to your own work

Most writers get their break from writing a 'spec script' (speculative script). This is a script that you are not paid for but which becomes your calling card. In this book I am going to assume that this script you are going to write is the pilot for a format you are creating, that you are the show runner and have to write the pilot episode and suggest further story outlines for future episodes. This is a technique I have used in workshop situations: getting a group of students to create an idea for a series, write key scenes from the first and fifth episodes, and, in some cases, film them. There is no better way to understand the process of episodic drama.

It is unlikely that creating a format will be your first TV writing assignment but an understanding of what is involved in putting together such a project is a great help when you are asked to write an individual episode for an established series. There will, of course, be diversions into other aspects of TV drama – the TV movie, for example – but if you have a thorough understanding of the mechanism of episodic drama formats, it will give you a solid basis to build on.

Of course not everybody will want to follow this book in the same way. The novice writer can work from chapter to chapter as he/she would pursue a course. The more experienced writer may want to spin through to the chapter headings, character, dialogue, etc., and pick and mix their own course, trouble-shooting areas where they have difficulty. TV is a popular medium and we watch it all the time, largely uncritically. Once you become a professional writer, although you hopefully never lose your ability to enjoy, a part of your brain will forever be thinking, 'How does that work?'.

The General Reader

The enormous growth in what I call 'scripturgy', that is the flood of attempts to formalize the principles of scriptwriting, has led to many books that are incomprehensible to the general reader. This also means they are often intimidating to the novice. The media generally, and television in particular, are prone to navel-gazing and jargon; I have tried not to lose sight of that general reader. Even if you've never read any scripturgy and have no intention of writing a script, I hope you will be able to enjoy this book.

In the Appendix I have provided a step outline of *The Shield*. There is also a Glossary, a short Bibliography and some useful websites.

Gender

Finally a note on gender. There are so many excellent female screenwriters in TV today, such as Linda La Plante, Caroline Aherne or Andrea Newman among hundreds of others. He/she contortions in this kind of book are stylistically uncomfortable, so from now on when I say 'he' of the screenwriter, I also mean 'she'.

WHAT MAKES A WRITER?

Writers are both born and made. Ideally they should be born with highly developed fantasy and imagination. They must be able to imagine stories and follow their fantasies, but they must discipline their imagination with observation. They must notice how people walk, talk, eat and make love. Writers who do not persist in their curiosity about the world soon burn out. We all have powers of observation but, as any policeman will tell you, we seldom use them to any acute degree. A programme like *Crimewatch* is dedicated to making people remember what they have seen. Observation on its own is useless unless you can put it to the service of storytelling. The best way to do this is to ask questions of what you see. This is the first step in dramatizing those questions as incidents.

You observe a man crying on a bus. Is he sad? Is he happy? Has he lost a child or become suddenly unemployed? Is he crying perhaps with happiness? An unexpected windfall or a romantic triumph? Is he faking? Is he trying to make someone believe he is sad? Is he perhaps just a chef who has been peeling too many onions. Invent his story. Ask yourself, 'How do I make people want to know this man's story?'.

WHAT MAKES A TV WRITER?

Given that you already have fantasy and imagination and are prepared to discipline and develop your observation, are there any unique qualities to being a TV writer? The TV writer should not be too concerned with immortality. Novelists, playwrights and screenwriters all tend to be better remembered and documented than such giants of TV writing as Paddy Chayevsky (*Marty*) and Nigel Kneal (*Quatermass*).

Writing On Sand

Writing for TV is writing on sand. In the UK in the seventies, much of the best early TV drama was wiped in a short-sighted attempt by both BBC and ITV (commercial television) to save money by re-using videotape. Analogue videotape decays, the surface can become fragile and powdery. I have sat in a session while an old drama of mine was painstakingly transferred to digital, five minutes at a time, with constant head cleaning and invisible edits to put together a digital version of the original play from the only crumbling copy in existence. Anybody who has tried to get a simple word-processing file written on outdated software read, will realize that speed of technological development and the ease with which data can be copied, paradoxically often makes it impermanent. There will be no Dead Sea Scrolls of TV drama.

TV writing is writing in the present tense for an incredibly voracious and greedy audience, whose very vices – inattention and ubiquity – are also their virtues. This is the trade-off. The literate vocal one per cent of the population who, in Great Britain, go to the theatre, may make more noise and merit many more column inches but the sometimes unsung TV writer can often slip his drama intravenously into the bloodstream of the nation. Also, as I will discuss later, a TV writer must sometimes surrender a portion of his ego. It is unusual for a writer, even if he is the show's creator (show runner), to have written a whole series on his own. However, writers like David Chase (*The Sopranos*) or Paul Abbot (*Shameless*) will, by a combination of creative recruitment and skilful script-editing, stamp their authorship on whole seasons of work that they have not actually written. The understanding you will gain about how other shows are constructed will help you when you come to work with characters and plots you have inherited. This process can make a bit of a dent in the expression of your cherished personal imagination; however, bringing your unique voice skilfully to a long-running series can often have dramatic results.

Here is how Gareth McClean *The Guardian* TV critic described the first episode of the sixth series of *Silent Witness*, a highly successful UK TV show starring Amanda Burton as a forensic pathologist:

> It soon became clear that *Silent Witness* had undergone a make-over – this wasn't just another demonstration of the talent of Amanda Burton and the uncomplicated decency of Professor Ryan. Written by Tony McHale this was an example of masterful story telling – fleet, economic and imminently watchable …. It was Sam Ryan as flawed heroine rather than Teflon Maverick. The prospect

of a struggle for redemption suddenly makes Sam's journey as a character worth watching.

In other words, a talented and highly experienced writer had given new depth to a very familiar character and so revitalized the series. In a similar way, when David Mamet wrote an episode for *Hill Street Blues* called *Wasted Weekend,* here is what John J. O'Connor said of it in *The New York Times*:

> The cast responds almost exuberantly to the hard-edged tone of the script. There is a pronounced lift to the performances. These are actors enjoying the challenge of new twists and insights. The lesson, not only for *Hill Street Blues* but also for any television series: there is nothing like an injection of strong, intelligent writing to get the adrenalin pumping again.

I believe very firmly in creative writing for TV. There is always room to invent, explore and entertain even in a medium that consistently gets a bad press.

> Every time you think television has hit its lowest ebb, a new programme comes along to make you wonder where you thought that ebb was.
>
> Art Buchwald

A punchy, rule-breaking episode is always possible and this challenge of re-inspiring is one that you will not find in any other kind of screenwriting. I also believe that the more you understand about the medium you are working in, and the more you test the boundaries of the particular writing assignment, then the more you can use the good aspects of them and transcend the bad.

TV in the UK and America

It has to be said at the outset that a direct comparison of UK TV and USA TV is like comparing a small cottage industry with a multi-national company. This leads to two connected faults in writing about TV: a jingoistic inferiority complex and a sense, on both sides, that 'they are doing it better'. In Britain we are able to make a series as quirky and original as *The Office*, while they can make a blockbuster like *Friends* that seems to sweep up audiences all over the world. I will not go down this cul-de-sac. I, of course, write from a UK perspective but I will pick examples from both sides of the Atlantic. This book is about creative writing for TV and the important thing is to celebrate it wherever it is found.

> We have as many networks as the US but they serve an audience only one-fifth the size. We also have Sky a broadcaster which is not so much a network as a platform, delivering many channels, but at a volume and with a turnover and technological advantage not matched by the US cable industry.
>
> Emily Bell, *The Guardian* 11 September 2006

Some Basic TV Formats

In the next chapter I will use the slightly funereal term 'laying out your script' rather than 'formatting your script' to avoid confusion. The reason for this is that when people who work in TV talk of 'formats' they mean the style or type of half-hour, hour, two-hour episodic drama that is under discussion. As in the sentence: 'The format of this show is half-hour comedy drama.' In TV the word 'format' has this specific meaning: game shows are formats, cop shows are formats. In the argot of TV, 'formats' fill 'slots' (*see* Glossary). There are also, of course, comedy formats and game-show formats. *Big Brother*, for example, is a reality TV show format; it first aired in the Netherlands in September 1999 but the format, with local variations, is now world-wide and the company that devised it, Endemol, has made millions from owning that format.

The basic building-block of TV drama tends to be the TV hour, which confusingly, because of commercial breaks, can last anything from forty-one minutes to fifty-nine minutes. Only the BBC and subscription channels like HBO can have the luxury of the sixty-minute hour! Even there, because of the necessity to think of foreign sales, you can often find the fifty-minute hour. Before we launch into this, we need to get straight in our mind two definitions:

- a serial is a drama told in parts, e.g. *Bleak House*;
- a series is a drama that is a different story each week, but has a core cast of characters and a basic location that stays the same, e.g. *Six Feet Under*, *Cheers* or *Casualty*.

The Two-Part Closed Serial

I use the term 'closed serial' to mean a story that comes to an end, even though it has several parts. The two-part closed serial is sometimes called a mini-series, though the term has rather fallen out of use. Generally it takes place over two consecutive evenings; on UK TV this is often Sunday and Monday night. The subject can vary. It may be based on a novel or be an original creation, it can be $2 \cdot 50$, $2 \cdot 70$ or even $2 \cdot 90$ minutes long. World-wide formats are legion and a production company will often have to produce, as part of their contract, a bewildering number of versions, not to mention tape formats. I asked an exceedingly experienced producer (Bill Shapter) to outline this for me; this is what he wrote – you may wish to take a deep breath before reading it!

> In some ways delivery to the networks has become simpler over the last few years. When digital tape formats first came in there was D1, a high quality intermediate D2 used by the ITV network, D3 used by the BBC, and D5 for Channel Five (no D4, as 4 is an unlucky number in Japan!), with secondary deliverables on low band U-Mat, and VHS copies. Nowadays all networks will take delivery on Digi-Beta, and/or high-definition tape depending on the acquisition medium (i.e. what the series was shot on), and any co-producer requirements, with viewing copies on

DVD. Normally one would have to deliver broadcast masters of the series, be it Digi Beta or HD or both, in three different screen ratios: 16 · 9 Full Height Anamorphic (FHA), 16 · 9 Letterbox and good old 4 · 3.

A series commissioned as 2 · 75, say, for domestic consumption, can often be required as 3 · 50 minutes for overseas sales, or as a cut down 120 minutes 'movie of the week', to be delivered in all the current tape formats and screen ratios above, and as NTSC copies, as opposed to PAL 625 lines at 50 cycles per second), if a sale is made to North America. Delivery items can be further complicated by the sound-track configurations required by different sales companies and distributors. Some copies will bear a fully mixed domestic version on tracks 1 and 2, with 'fully filled' dialogue-less music and effects track on tracks 3 and 4. Also time-coded separate dialogue, music and effects, (DMandE) tracks may be required, to enable trailers and promos to be cut to different broadcasters' specifications. Any parts of the original programme that carries English titles over picture material in the domestic version must also be supplied as 'textless'.

(525 lines 60 cycles per second).
See – simple.

As I said, a technical medium.

The two-part closed serial can also swell to three parts and so linger on into Tuesday night or even hang over into the following week. Given that the narrative can be chopped about in this way, a writer could get very confused trying to apply the traditional three-act structure to a drama that is basically built up from fifty-minute blocks or sections.

The Six or More Part Closed Serial

Again a story with a beginning, a middle and an end but told over six or more weeks. This unashamedly steals both the clothes and, often in an adaptation, the body of the novel. It mimics the novel's timetable. You view it as you read a novel over several weeks. It becomes a case, not of staying in for one or at the most two extra nights, but of making a permanent date in your diary every week; increasingly technology will do this for you. It obviously requires a degree of commitment from the viewer. The writer has the opportunity to develop character and indeed tackle time in a much more challenging way than would be possible over a mere two nights. If successful these serials can become weekly events. It was not so long ago that whole families sat down regularly to follow the twists and turns of David Lynch's *Twin Peaks* (1990) or Andrew Davies' adaptation of Jane Austen's *Pride and Prejudice* (1995).

The One-Hour Drama Series

This is a number of self-contained episodes. Each week a new story is told within the broadcast hour. Within that hour, the plot will have a beginning, a middle and an end, but the writers will bring to this week's story, serial elements: these will be story strands that the audience are familiar with, because they know the characters from previous weeks. For example, in an episode of *ER* (NBC 1994), nurse Ally's love-life or struggle with alcoholism would inform her actions and emotions in the plot of the week's drama. Even though she is not the main protagonist, and even if her problems are not directly relevant to this week's episode, her history will inform our view of her. Our appreciation of the drama will be enriched by our memory of the character's life from past episodes and our expectations for them in future episodes. The long-range control of these serial elements within a series is called storylining, which we will discuss later.

The Soap

> By soap opera I mean a continuous serial of contemporary life, where traditional moral values are asserted. Each episode in a soap opera advances the plots and sub-plots, but does not resolve them (that is what series do: serials drag it out as long as possible).
>
> Peter Buckman, *All for Love*, 1984

The soap episode is generally thirty minutes long but can extend over many months, even years. It can be on three, four or five nights a week. It has a cast of characters generally grouped around a single location, e.g. Albert Square for *EastEnders*, Brookside Close for *Brookside*. Its history – the document or database that records this – is called 'The Bible'; it may go back thirty years or more.

The Bible. In many ways, the true custodians of the bible of a soap are not so much the script editors as the audience. The fans have often grown up with it and can even date significant moments in their lives with reference to historic events in their favourite soap. I remember one woman telling me that she had had a car crash, 'The night when Angie [a character in the British soap *EastEnders*] took the pills'. The real life event was dated by the calendar of the fictional suicide. These iconic soap moments fix in fans' brains in ways that more real anniversaries may not.

The bible of a long-running soap has become a collective memory, a backstory that the fans share and feel that they own. It has become the nearest thing we have to the myths that provided the shared sense of community that made Greek tragedy possible. However, the soaps' dramatic roots are not in Greek tragedy, they are rather in popular and populist entertainments like melodrama, where the peaks of dramatic action were high-lighted by frantic scoring; frantic scoring remaining a feature of soaps to this day.

TV movies, serials and high-budget series are generally shot on film or high-definition videotape but soaps are almost always made on videotape with multi-camera set-ups used to facilitate the recording of a lot of material per day. The British soap *EastEnders* shoots thirteen minutes a day on the lot (Albert Square) and fifteen to sixteen minutes in the studio. A TV film would probably average between three and five minutes a day.

Soaps are enormously popular, they present the viewer with a heightened version of everyday life. Whatever your troubles, soaps will dramatize them in many and varied ways. They seem to be answering the question, 'How do we live our lives now?'. They seem to lose their audience when, however tenuous their line to reality is, it snaps.

> Earth calling *Brookside*. Earth calling *Brookside*. Please phone home.
> 'Tapehead' column in Guardian TV Guide, 1996

So 'Tapehead', AKA critic Jim Shelley pleaded with the UK TV series creator Phil Redmond. The line had snapped and so like an airship that had lost its moorings, *Brookside* began its slow drift into extinction.

Soaps are comparatively cheap and they consistently provide top ratings for schedulers so, pound for pound, they are therefore the most effective kind of UK TV drama. In Chapter 7 I will deal at length with soaps – it is, inevitably, the longest chapter!

Half-Hour Sit-Com

The half-hour situation comedy is also barely twenty-three minutes long, and is often a tape drama shot in permanent sets consisting of a few rooms, e.g. *Men Behaving Badly* (UK) before a live audience. There will sometimes be some exterior filmed or taped inserts and these will be played to the studio audience so their laughter can be recorded. These half-hours are distinct from the longer comedy dramas like *Only Fools and Horses* and *One Foot in The Grave*, where the action spreads into further settings and the occasional exterior sequence. These anyway are generally an hour long and because of that tend to have more developed story lines. The comedy is more dependent on character and less reliant on a minimum of two gags a page.

I have written Chapter 10 on comedy because comic TV writing is one of the UK's glories and because I think there are seriously useful lessons for any writer to learn from comedy writing.

These then are the basic kinds of episodic TV drama. Naturally, dramas put into episodes and subdivided by commercial breaks can always be split and split again. International sales can often lead to subdivisions of the drama that were never thought of by the original writers and producers. For example, a UK police drama, when shown in France, can be re-cut to squeeze it into a single night. The reason being that that's the way the French broadcast cop shows.

However, leaving aside the thirty-minute soap and the sit-com, the basic building block of even a three-evening episodic piece, and this also applies to extended comedy dramas, is the one-hour (fifty-two minute) section. As a unit of drama it is in many ways harder than the ninety-minute to two-hour feature film and most often has to be written with the knowledge that it will be broken up by commercial breaks.

The audience for an episodic drama can often know the characters in a series better than the novice writer of the current episode. Unlike the movie audience, they require different things. Already hooked by previous episodes, they demand to be led into new pastures that do not corrupt, at least irrevocably, a character they know and love.

Structural 'rules' should always be regarded as channel markers. The way to approach the constraints of episodic writing, inherited characters, the series bible or writing as a member of a team, is analogous. There may be rather more channel markers in a series but you as a writer are still in control of the ship!

In this book my touchstone will be how good writers have approached plot, character, dialogue, time and so on. They will be the guides to the aspiring TV writer. TV now has a history but I will only look back at that history in order to look forward into the future. In any case, the future, in TV terms, is seldom further imagined than the day after tomorrow.

2 THE TV SCRIPT AND HOW TO LAY IT OUT

The formatting of scripts has become a lot easier since the advent of scriptwriting software like Final Draft (www.finaldraft.com). These applications make the apparently bizarre rules of capitalization and spacing that students often find perplexing and could tax even a skilled word-processor automatic. The advice is to use one of these software programs. You can download free demos of most of them from the Net. If you cannot afford one of these, slavishly copy the example below.

I would stress two things, many of the greatest TV scripts were written without screenwriting software. Dennis Potter wrote in long-hand and Alan Bleasdale bashed out *Boys From The Blackstuff* on an Imperial typewriter. Any competent person who uses Microsoft Word all the time can actually set up tabs and macros for you that will create the basic margins you need at the touch of a function key. If you have such a friend, this is worth half an hour and the cost of a few drinks. Failing that, the excellent BBC writer's website (www.bbc.co.uk/writersroom) provides *Script Smart*, which is a handy series of macros that will effectively turn Microsoft Word into a screenwriting program. The site also has excellent instructions on how to present and submit a script to the BBC.

Your spec script (see below) will not be rejected if a margin is a little out but it is vital that you present it cleanly and neatly. Readers are often tired and have read several scripts at a sitting – you do not want yours to be the one that exasperates them by its illegibility. Scripts are not easy to read for they are trying to convey the effect of a finished product that will combine dialogue, picture and music to tell a story. So give yourself the best chance you can by presenting it well.

A plain typed script, well bound and without any fancy gimmicks, such as multi-coloured covers or flashy pictures, will, at the initial stage, be enough. Leave it to your producer to spend money on any presentation that he or she might like to make. In almost all cases the layout suggested below will suffice. If a producer requires some other format, ask him about it before you deliver.

The latest version of *Final Draft 7* has nine screenplay formats, three stage-play formats, text documents and ninety-three examples of TV scripts. However, all of these examples represent slight variations on the basic script pattern shown below. Our computers now do much of this formatting for us,

18

so I have given the reasons for the various margins and so on. Even if this information becomes lost in the mist of the pre-digital age, you will know why scripts look the way they do.

SCENE-BASED SCREENPLAY

Below is an example of a script layout – *Baby Love* adapted by Tony Bicât from the novel by Denise Danks. This is the basic screenplay format and the one that, unless otherwise directed, you should use.

Font: Courier New 12 (the Final Draft default setting). Using this font in conjunction with standard screenplay format enables readers to time your script, using the rule of thumb that one page equals one minute of screen time. 'Silent' pages, i.e. pages containing nothing but action, may play shorter but will be balanced by other pages filled with dialogue.

Spacing: Your basic setting is single spacing. This applies to: action, character name and dialogue. Insert a double carriage return between scene headings and action and between scenes.

Page numbering: top right for easy reference

Scene numbering: If you are not using screenwriting software, where it is only a matter of a couple of key strokes, number scenes only in the final draft of a script, placing numbers either side of the scene heading. Scene numbering makes collaboration easier, but it is not vital.

Scene heading (aka slug line): This is always in upper case, so that you instantly know where you are – it is therefore easy for production to count the number of times you use a location.

A Note on *Movie Magic*

Final Draft is compatible with *Movie Magic*, this budgeting and scheduling software is very much an industry standard. If your slug line looks like this:

INT. GEORGINA'S FLAT/THE BATHROOM – DAY

Then *Movie Magic* will read it with ease. If, however, you write it like this:

INT - GEORGINA'S FLAT. THE BATHROOM/DAY

Then whoever is doing the budget will have to correct the dots and dashes or *Movie Magic* will think your dash is a location!

INT. = interior or indoors: Any scene where the characters are inside, whether it is an aircraft hangar, a toilet or a car.

Note INT should be followed by a full stop.

EXT. = exterior or outdoors: Any scene where the characters are outside like a patio, a street or the Siberian steppe.

1 INT GEORGINA'S FLAT THE **OFFICE-BEDROOM DAY.** 1

Suddenly Girl growls. There is the noise of a motorbike. It
roars up and parks outside.

Georgina lies flat on the floor beside girl. The helmetted
figure of The Dispatch Rider, carrying a package, climbs up
to ring Richard's front door. George is certain it's the
bomber. His metalled boots ring on the concrete steps like a
death knell.

      GEORGINA
   Don't open it.

Upstairs the Dispatch Rider rings the bell. Georgina sees her
phone over the other side of the room.

         CUT TO:

2 INT RICHARD'S FLAT DAY 2

Richard struggling to get off the bed . The door bell ringing
insistently.

3 INT GEORGINA'S FLAT OFFICE BEDROOM DAY 3

Georgina crawling across the floor towards her phone .

4 INT RICHARD'S FLAT DAY 4

Richard now lurching across the room to get to his crutches.

5 EXT FRONT DOOR OF RICHARD'S HOUSE DAY. 5

The Dispatch Rider gives up he puts a card through the box.

6 INT RICHARD'S FLAT DAY 6

Richard sees the card flutter to the floor as, painfully
slowly, he hobbles across the hall.

7 INT GEORGINA'S FLAT OFFICE BEDROOM DAY 7

Georgina scrabbling to her phone as in the street the bike
roars away.

8 INT RICHARD'S FLAT DAY 8

Richard looking at the card. Answering his phone.

      RICHARD
   It was for you. I wish you'd tell
   people you've moved downstairs -
   you could at least have shouted up
   to him.
     (MORE)

Note EXT should be followed by a full stop.

DAY is self-explanatory and can be replaced by NIGHT for a scene that happens at night.

Action ('business'): Keep visual and concise. Remember that your descriptive style is an integral element of the story's appeal. Do not include passages that describe the life of the character's mind or the quality of his perceptions – these belong in novels. Avoid lengthy descriptions of characters' appearance and dress. What do we see? What do the characters do?

The reason the action margins are indented (set in) is to differentiate them at a glance from the more deeply indented dialogue margins.

Characters' names: Capitalize these when they first appear. Thereafter they may be rendered in lower case, though you have the option of capitalizing them throughout. The reason for this is so that actors and production can easily see when a new character enters the action.

Dialogue: This is further indented with the character's name centred in caps over that dialogue. The reason for this is that actors can clearly see which lines they have to speak and production can easily count how many scenes a certain actor is in. However, characters' names are never capitalized in the dialogue itself.

Significant sounds: CREAKS, BLASTS, the phone RINGING – are capitalized.

Parentheses: Use sparingly to qualify dialogue when necessary but do not write action in parentheses. For example:

LINDA

(sarcastically) You really know how to woo a girl ...
(she stares at the wilted bunch of garage flowers)

DAVE

(kicks off his loafers and starts to unbutton his shirt)
    I'm due back at 2.00 ...

Instead write:

LINDA

(sarcastically) You really know how to woo a girl ...

She stares at the wilted bunch of garage flowers as Dave kicks off his loafers and starts to unbutton his shirt.

DAVE

I'm due back at 2.00 ...

Transitions: Avoid littering your script with 'cut to', 'dissolve to' unless you feel that specifying the type of transition is absolutely necessary.

Page breaks: When a scene continues across a page break write 'CONTINUED' bottom-right and '(CONTINUED)' top-left of the next page, preceded by the scene number, if applicable. For example:

75. (CONTINUED)

Standard rules for dialogue that continues over a page break are:

- do not separate dialogue from the character's name;
- break after at least two lines;
- break at end of sentence;
- insert '(MORE)' on the next line;
- repeat the name at the top of the next page followed by '(cont'd)'.

Bindings

Comb bindings enable the pages to lie flat. A script bound with brads ('blodgers') is forever trying to spring closed, which can be an irritant, especially for someone who has to read a lot of scripts. However, if submitting commissioned work, ask the producer, script exec or whoever if he wants the pages loose or bound with brads for ease of copying.

The script should be bound either with a card binder or acetate, which protects from coffee and other fluids. Unbound scripts swiftly deteriorate, with the title page coming to resemble a poppadum.

Colour graphics on a dedicated title page can look sexy, or they can seem like a gimmick to snag the attention. Since they are usually added when the script is locked off and packaged up, they suggest that you regard the script as finished. Is it? Almost certainly not!

Always read what you write aloud to someone before you submit it. Can they follow it and understand it easily?

Make sure that your Agent's details, or your own are on the title page. And never ever send your only copy. This is all you need to know about laying out and submitting your script.

Five Rules

- Unless you are asked to do otherwise, lay out your script in basic screenplay format.
- Make sure your script is clear and legible.
- Make sure it is securely bound.
- Make sure your name or your agent's name, address, telephone number and e-mail is on the cover.
- Always retain a copy, never ever send the only copy.

OTHER TYPES OF SCRIPT LAYOUT

You may also come across other types of script layout. These generally relate to aspects of production. It is interesting to look at these. As a writer you will not be asked to format your script like this but they illustrate the essential problem of script writing: namely that you must convey, merely with the written word, the effects of picture, sound and design. Grappling with this translation of the page to the screen is what production is all about. The more you understand how a page translates to picture, then the better grasp you will have of the medium. There are many writers who prefer to remain in ignorance of this process. If you are one of these skip to the next chapter.

Comedy Scripts

Comedy scripts sometimes have the action in capitals, this is because the humour can often be in the action as much as in the dialogue. American comedy scripts, and some TV scripts for multi-camera studio shows, have the action in capitals and are double-spaced. A double-spaced script will time at one and a half pages a minute.

Camera Scripts (Tech Scripts in the USA)

As a writer you will not have to write these but it is useful to know what they look like. If your script comes back laid out on one side of the page only, with an ultra-wide margin it is a good thing. Those empty spaces are for the camera instructions (see below), they are a sign that you are nearing production.

In multi-camera work, studio or outside broadcast, the camera instructions are written on the left, the action and dialogue on the right.

21. 2   ADDISON: Shut up/ I'm thinking.
    H/A 2/S Pete, Addison   Should we inform the police?
                         (Pause) Then there's the press, two
                         number ones in two months if he
                         farts he's news ...

22. 1   GESTURES/
    MCU Pete   PETE: (NERVOUS) Funny how you
                         sweat your guts out trying to get
                         press coverage and then you get a
                         chance at unlimited column inches
                         and that's

23. 2   the last thing you want./
    MCU Addison

                         SHOT 24 CAM 1 NEXT

Note the abbreviations: H/A = High Angle; MCU = Medium Close Up.

Story Synopsis

These can be anything from half a page to twenty pages, generally four pages would be enough. You should have a title page and put the log line (*see* Glossary), on the front as well as you or your agent's details.

Character Breakdowns

These are often asked for. They can be from six lines to a full page for major protagonist. Put the name of the character as a heading.

EVE DOVE

Martin's daughter, a tyro TV reporter, who is beginning to make a name for herself. Attractive and curious by nature, she seems born for the job she does. Doubtless it has not hurt her to have a famous father but she is not uncritical of him. She has barely curbed a rebellious and maverick streak that she got from her mother who died when she was young.

Bibles and Series' Synopses

There are no golden rules as to how these should be set out but clear headings, concise and not too flowery descriptions are good rules to follow.

In 1998, Nigel McCreery, the successful creator of several long-running British TV series, among them *Silent Witness*, and I were asked by Pearson TV to come up with an idea for a series set on The Isle of Man. The bible of *Baxter*, as it was called, contained:

- a log line;
- half-page synopsis of basic series idea;
- character breakdowns of all major characters;
- synopses of six episodes;
- background historical and geographical detail of the island;
- a family tree showing the relationships of the various characters.

It ran to thirty pages and was submitted together with the first draft of the two-hour pilot entitled *Mad Sunday*.

Story Boards

However badly you draw, I would always advise writers to doodle storyboards when trying to write complicated sequences. You don't have to be Rembrandt and, if they embarrass you, you don't have to show them to anyone but it is surprising how often a problem that you can't work out with words, you can with pictures.

Shot Lists and Shot-Based Screenplays

These are much more the province of the writer/director. Shot lists are a list of the shots that a director wishes to make for a particular sequence. They are generally not in story order.

1. MS (medium or mid-shot). Richard on the bed, he struggles with his crutches.
2. CU (close up). Richard's point of view of the letter box.

3. MS (medium or mid-shot). Georgina crawling across floor of the flat.
4. BCU (big close up). Georgina's terrified eyes.

Although a writer would never put a shot list in a script, it's sometimes useful when thinking about a scene to try to imagine what shots would be necessary to complete it.

Shot-based screenplays are scripts that contain detailed directorial instructions. They are not often used in television outside commercials; however, if you are stuck, they can be a useful tool to help you imagine a sequence. As an exercise let us examine what Georgina's flat scene would look like written out as a shot-based screenplay. The story board for this sequence is shown on pages 27–28.

1: TRACK the sinister boots of the dispatch rider up the steps, his leathers, his sinister helmet.
2: JIB and PAN to his gloved hand as he rings the bell.
3: MEDIUM SHOT (MS) In the flat below, Georgina, convinced the despatch rider is the bomber, lunges for her phone. She trips and the phone skeeters across the room, to wedge itself under a chest of drawers.
4: Her Point of View (POV) of the falling phone.
5: CAMERA HANDHELD lurches with Richard, his leg in plaster, struggles off the bed. The doorbell ringing insistently.
6: CLOSE UP (CU) of Georgina's face as she strains to reach the phone.
7: CLOSE UP (CU) of Richard as he lopes unevenly on the crutches to the door.
8: His POINT OF VIEW (POV) of the closed door and the letter box.
9: MEDIUM SHOT (MS) of the despatch rider reaching into his coat for something we cannot see.
10: MEDIUM SHOT (MS) of frantic Georgina reaching for the phone, fumbling as she dials Richard.
11: CLOSE UP (CU) as the dispatch rider puts something we can't see through the letter box.
12: CLOSE UP (CU) as Georgina almost screams into the phone.

GEORGINA

Don't open the door!

13: Richard's POV of card dropping through door as he answers the phone.
14: MEDIUM SHOT (MS) of Richard juggling phone and crutches while reading the card.

RICHARD

I wish you'd bloody tell people you've moved.

15: LONG SHOT (L/S) of Georgina kneeling on floor, shaking and sobbing with relief.

Don't present your script like this but thinking carefully about the shots can help you in creating it. The challenge is to write the sequence in such a way that even though you lay out your script in the standard screenplay format, the Final Draft default setting described in the first part of the chapter, its eventual realization will mirror the shots you have worked out in your head or doodled in your story board.

It is not that you wish to pre-empt the director but, particularly in action sequences, the more carefully you have worked them out, then the more confidently you will write them. This in turn means that, even though their final staging does not follow your plan, the sequence will end up being more powerful on screen.

THE CALLING-CARD SCRIPT

The script that signals your arrival, that draws the attention of a producer to your writing is your calling card. This script for the novice writer is always a 'spec script', that is a speculative script that you have not been paid for. Producers want to know that you can write and the only way they can find this out is to read examples of your work. You must have them ready. Sometimes they will ask you to try write an episode of their series but more often than not a good example of your writing, a play or a short story even, can be what gains their interest. There are famous examples of writers who impressed with an unmade, even an un-filmable, script but no examples of writers who have impressed without a script.

If you are trying to join a writing team and your spec script is accepted, it will almost certainly be re-written by other hands, so you may well be tempted to ask, 'Why bother? Why should I polish and re-polish it, if it will be almost totally re-written?'. The answer is that your calling-card script speaks for you. You may be a genius but if your script is hard to read and lazily presented, ask yourself, 'Are these the qualities a producer would like to work with?'. The answer is of course, 'No', so give yourself the best chance you can. Professional presentation indicates a professional attitude. It says: 'This is someone we may be able to work with.'

FURTHER INFORMATION

BBC: www.bbc.co.uk/writersroom
Final Draft: www.finaldraft.com
Writer's Guild Of America: www.wga.org
Writers Guild Of Great Britain: www.writersguild.org.uk

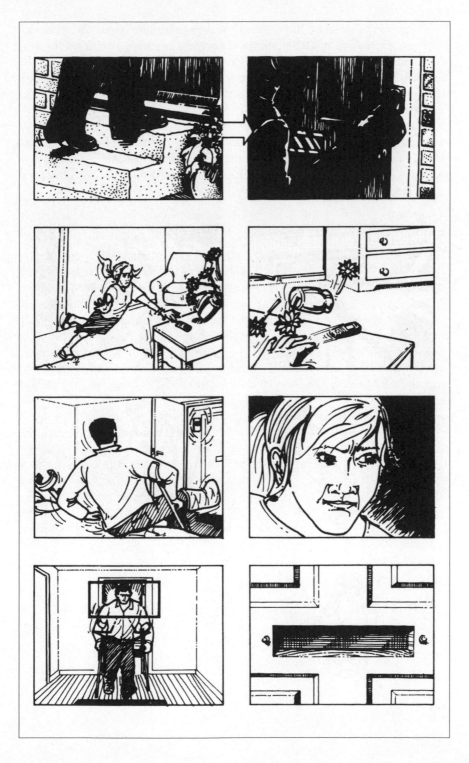

3 PILOT

If you are to write for TV, what kind of worlds must you be prepared to immerse yourself in? And why should those worlds be any different from the worlds of the feature film or the stage play? Do those worlds have any particular characteristics? What can we learn from them?

In this chapter I will examine a famous pilot episode to show how it approaches plot, character and the world of the story. It is important that the TV writer, as well as nurturing his imagination and disciplining his fantasy with observation, explores and analyses what is on TV. The most useful tool to help you watch creatively is the step outline. What is a step outline?

STEP OUTLINE

A step outline is a document that deconstructs a screenplay or a film (TV episode) by laying out the action in sequential narrative steps. It allows us to see the spine of the plot.

Plot is character in action. Dialogue can be seductive but if you restrict yourself to a few words of dialogue as a heading (*see* the step outline of *The Shield* on page 131), you can focus on how the plot works.

Making a step outline has become much easier with the advent of DVD. The ability to navigate through a DVD in chapters has, in the same way that non-linear editing has simplified the mechanics of film and tape editing, made making a step outline less of a chore. A step outline exposes the bare bones of the story. It is a document that, unlike the script, which may contain seductive dialogue and well-written scenes that divert the reader, reveals the skeleton of the plot. It is therefore not a selling document but a tool for writers and producers to examine what exactly they have. A step outline will often show you that that fabulous scene, that terrific speech, may be in the wrong place or even the wrong show! In the USA a step outline is called a 'beat sheet'. It follows the beats in a story; that is, those moments when the action changes gear. You will be able to follow these in Chapter 4 when we discuss *Prime Suspect*. You can also, as an exercise, follow the step outline of *The Shield*, which is in the Appendix, while watching the DVD.

You can use step outlines to learn from broadcast shows and to strip down and repair your own script. You will also find that when you start working with a group of writers on an extended story line (*see* below) the technique of working with a step outline/beat sheet will prove to be invaluable.

HILL STREET BLUES – EPISODE ONE

Hill Street Blues was written by Steven Bochco and premiered on NBC TV on Jan 15 1981 – it really did change the face of TV drama. It introduced and created a bunch of characters and a milieu that, with certain changes, maintained a consistent hold on viewers through a seven-season run of 146 one-hour episodes between 1981 and 1987.

It created what came to be called 'precinct drama'. This is a drama of many characters, whose interlocking personal lives interact with a weekly story around a fixed location. This was both economically sound, a permanent reusable set saves money, but also imaginatively coherent and inherently satisfying. It showed writers and producers a new way to make TV drama.

Hill Street Blues had many other qualities. It was realistic, well-researched and witty. Many of the characters were flawed and led complicated lives and, although their basic business was the solving of crime, it plunged the viewer each week into the drama, not only of the crimes but of the policemen and women's lives. Few of its subsequent imitators have ever got near it. It also had a great theme tune and even a catch phrase, when the avuncular Sergeant Phil Esterhaus sent the cops on the way with 'Hey – let's be careful out there'.

Recognition

The theme tune and catch phrase of *Hill Street Blues* are not small things. One of the most important tasks for the TV writer is to create an instantly recognizable presence – a brand, if you like. The tone of *Hill Street Blues* was flawless: as soon as you switched on, you recognized it, you knew where you were. This quality of instant identification has to come from the writing. A sexy title sequence won't do it, nor will the catch phrase and title music on its own. As channels proliferate and our 'grazing' viewing habits increase, our attachment to a series – be it by style or by character – becomes more and more important. I will examine this point further in future chapters.

Policemen have always been good subjects for drama. 'Sharp-end activities', that is jobs which deal with life and death, firemen, doctors and spies, naturally lend themselves to exciting story lines. Over the years the police have moved from the cosy reassurance of *Dixon of Dock Green* (GB 1955) to being little better than the criminals (*The Shield* USA 2002). This is not the place to study this progression or what it says about our society, but we have perhaps a need to use the dramatic representation of the police to externalize our fears on a fairly regular basis.

The Pilot

Episode one of *Hill Street Blues* is also a pilot. If you initiate a TV series, you have to write a pilot; that is, the first episode that will both pitch and set the tone of what is to come. In the UK we do not tend to make pilots, since our series are so much shorter. (Contrast the 33 episodes of *Inspector Morse* (UK) with the 146 of *Hill Street Blues*.) That said, often a single drama will get made in the UK with a central character who seems specifically designed to have series potential. In the US, for example, in 2005, Fox Drama took 350 drama pitches, commissioned 60 scripts, made 8 pilots of which 3 went to series and only one was a hit. Most companies hope to get one hit every couple of years. (Source: Paul Jackson, *LA Stories*, a BBC radio programme of 2006.)

Still, the idea of the pilot episode is a good one for you to keep in mind. If you are trying to get work as a TV writer, the fact that you have written a single drama, which suggests a character or characters that might have series potential, as well as demonstrating a clear one-hour story arc, it shows your story could have long-term possibilities. This is more likely to convince a producer that you have the skills to work in episodic drama.

Hill Street Station, Episode one of *Hill Street Blues*, is an exemplary pilot, so I will analyse it in detail. The way I do this will also serve as a blueprint for the technique you can use to examine other shows for yourself. Remember that any analysis you do will be much more valuable for your creative development as a writer than anything you read in a book.

HILL STREET BLUES

A caption reads 'Hill Street Station'. This is the title of the episode and also tells us where we are. There is no conventional establishing shot. We go straight into roll call.

1. *Hey, be careful out there.*
   Sgt Phil Esterhaus hands out assignments as the unruly and scruffy police gossip. Old ladies are having purses snatched and there is humour at the description of a transvestite purse-snatcher. The cops only fall silent at the mention of gang homicides – two last night. There is a directive about unauthorized weapons being produced. A table is soon covered with an assortment of flick knives, concealed guns and so on. Esterhaus sends them on their way with the lines that will become the catchphrase of the series, 'Let's roll – hey, be careful out there'. The cops collect up their unauthorized weapons.
2. *Respect for an officer of the law.*
   Hill and Renko are discussing Hill's domestic arrangements and Renko's new silver-inlaid cowboy boots, which give him height. They are passed by a pimp and three whores being brought in by Belker. The tallest of the three whores pushes the diminutive Renko aside. Renko is outraged and protests. Belker snarls at the pimp.

Credits.

> 4 minutes and 36 seconds in and a unit (police car) rolls out of the underground garage of Hill Street Station and we get stills of the main protagonist and the names of the actors who play them.

In this first sequence most of the main players are glimpsed and we get stills of the others in the credits. There is no establishing shot (*see* Glossary). In this case it would be an exterior of Hill Street Station. We go straight in and become involved, both with the crimes, the homicides and purse-snatchings, and with Hill and Renko's personal lives. The display of unauthorized weapons tells us that, although the atmosphere is light even witty, these cops deal with violence on a daily basis. Belker's attack dog personality is set up. It's very compressed and economical.

3. *Interface with the police experience.*
A man and a woman scrap in the holding room, while Furillo talks to an education official on the phone. He then reprimands two officers for hitting a suspect with a board. They say they just did it to get his attention. He gives them money to buy the guy breakfast and pacify him. Joyce Davenport, a defence lawyer, barges in. She demands that they release her client. She harangues Furillo as the cops watch. Esterhaus says that her client is lost somewhere between the station and the courthouse. Furillo persuades her to wait. John LaRue, a good-looking cop who fancies himself, comes on to her over the coffee machine. She does not stop him fingering her gold chain. Is she attracted to him? (9.05)

4. *'My hair is down'.*
As Davenport warns Furillo that he must find her client or risk charges, a suspect grabs a knife from the unauthorized weapons table, and goes berserk. Five cops restrain him, while others restrain Belker, who wants to bite the guy's ankle. He protests that just because two years ago he bit off a suspect's nose, everybody is down on him. Joyce watches sardonically. La Rue hovers attentively explaining he can't help in the scuffle as he is undercover. As the suspect is held in a headlock, Lucille, a female cop, calms him saying they will take him to hospital. Johnnie leads Joyce away. He asks her what she is like with her hair down. She replies acidly that it is down.

Furillo is presented as defusing a potentially difficult situation and also doing three things at once. The gorgeous Joyce Davenport shows herself totally unfazed by the macho station environment and it is significant that policewoman Lucille persuades the berserk suspect to come quietly, wittily rebuking a colleague for copping a feel of her breasts in the ruck. These women handle the male-dominated world with assurance.

5. *My two-year-old is stopping smoking.*
Inside Hill and Renko's car they are talking about their love lives. They stumble on a liquor store robbery. (13.05) There are gunshots. Police with guns bursting through the swing doors inside the station. Furillo and Esterhaus on phones saying that they don't yet know if it's a hostage situation. (13.46) Henry Goldblum, a negotiator, is on a pay phone in a nearby store trying to get the exchange to connect him to the liquor store

phone so he can talk with the guys doing the hold-up. The operator demands that he pay for the call. While searching for change, he sticks a child's dummy in his mouth. His partner asks him if he is teething or just stopping smoking. (15.14)

6. *We need crowd control.*
The cops are barely able to restrain a big crowd that has gathered outside the liquor store. Belker spots a bald-headed pickpocket taking an old lady's purse. He goes in pursuit. (15.46)

7. *No one's been hurt yet.*
Back to Goldblum talking to hostages who are two nervous Puerto Rican kids. He tries to calm them. Hector, the leader of the two, demands to speak to Jesus Martinez, the war lord of the youth gang Los Diabolos.

> We are seeing the world from inside the cop car thinking of Hill and Renko's lives when they stumble across a dramatic and dangerous incident. After the hail of gunfire that greets them, there is a time jump as we go back to the commotion at the station. We remain inside the various locations and the focus is on the characters and their feelings, rather than milking the action. This illustrates a point I will expand on later – story point of view (SPOV). Through whose eyes are we seeing/living this? How you tell a story depends on the answer to this question. Once they are shot, we cease to be in Hill and Renko's Story POV but are back in the story POV of the cops in Hill Street Station.

> Next, we are introduced to a new character, Henry Goldblum, and of course learn that he has a two-year-old. We also meet the two Puerto Rican kids holding up the store. They appear young and nervous but dangerously armed.

8. *'No one's been hurt yet.'*
Back to Goldblum talking to hostages, who are two nervous Puerto Rican kids. He tries to calm them. Hector, the leader of the two, demands to speak to Jesus Martinez, the warlord of the youth gang Los Diabolos.

9. *A roll of kosher toilet paper.*
Back at the station, Furillo is arguing with Howard Hunter, who leads the Emergency Action Team, that the cops prefer to call EAT, much to Howard's annoyance. This is Howard's swat team. Howard wants to go in hard, show these punks who is boss. He says that Goldblum couldn't defuse a roll of kosher toilet paper. Again, Furillo is all for negotiation and the peaceful approach. Howard, however, is gung-ho and borderline racist. (18.51)

> The brief exterior sequence of the cops crouching by their cars is followed by Goldblum trying to negotiate and the confrontation between Furillo and Howard Hunter. The focus is on the antagonism between these two, their very different police methods. Hunter is set up as a bit of a ridiculous figure. However, he does manage to persuade Furillo to let him deploy his hardware. It's clear he despises Furillo as a bit of a pussy.

10. *We've all been there.*

Fay, Furillo's ex-wife, enters. She is in a fury. Furillo's alimony cheque bounced and he took their son to a ball game when he had a temperature. Esterhaus steers her away. Furillo apologizes to Gomez. Fay asks Phil Esterhaus how his wife of twenty-three years, Margaret, is. He says they have split up and tells her of his teenage sweetheart Cindy. Fay disguises her laughter by burying her face in her handkerchief. Velker brings in the bald purse snatcher. (21:55)

11. *Mom no crying ...*

As the tough Velker is laboriously typing with one finger, logging in the bald pickpocket, Richard T Wilton, he gets a call from his mother. As he argues with her, she gives him a bad time; she is even crying into his ear. The pickpocket can barely restrain his laughter. Belker snarls at him but his tough guy image has been dented. (23:41) Fay has a final go at Furillo. Their son is being counselled by the shrink she is dating. Furillo thinks this is unethical. He says he will cover the cheque but now he has an important meeting. Fay is unimpressed when it turns out to be with three teenage street kids, the leader of whom is Jesus Hermenez.

Despite this tense situation, Furillo has to deal with his furious ex-wife Fay. We learn about cuddly Phil Esterhaus's teenage squeeze and the shrink that Fay is dating. We learn that Velker is as soft as butter when he is on the phone to mom. As Fay watches Jesus and his bodyguards, we get the strong sense that the women in this show think these cops are not serious. They are just fooling around in several senses.

12. *Exterior of the building. A police car drives past. (24:42)*

Food is brought in by a reluctant Esterhaus for the kids. Furillo tries to get Jesus to help defuse the hostage situation. The street leader makes extravagant demands but settles for a cop car and a flak jacket for Hermenez's mother to be taken through rival gangland territory to the clinic. A deal.

It is nearly half way in before we get this clear establishing shot of Hill Street Station. The concentration is on the antagonism of the cops to the uppity street kids. The cops all look as if they want to beat them senseless and fling them into the street but Furillo goes against this and forces what looks like a deal with Jimenez.

13. *No wonder this country is rotting.*

There is a high shot of the police cars surrounding the stake out. Negotiations in progress but Hunter and his helicopters and SWAT team, who rejoice in the comic acronym EAT, have arrived on the scene. (24:45)

Hunter ridicules Goldblum's attempts at negotiation.

14. *At the station.*

Hector and Jesus row and cut off the negotiations Jesus walks out. Furillo talks to Hector and says he is coming over to negotiate in person. Gomez takes over the phone and talks in Spanish to Hector. Furillo leaves. (30:46)

15. *If she turns you down ...*

La Rue calls Joyce Davenport and lies to her that her suspect is at the station. He reckons when she comes over, by the time she finds out that the suspect is not there, La Rue will be able to take her to a fancy restaurant. His partner Neal Washington senses that Davenport is way out of La Rue's class.

> The stakeout looks as if it is heading for a violent conclusion unless Furillo can save the day. The subplot of La Rue's attempt to seduce Davenport is kept going, providing a light-hearted counterpoint to this tense situation. This is a good example of the writers keeping all the balls in the air. It is also useful to note the economy of the expensive establishing shots. (The high shot of the cop cars that starts this sequence.) The way shots of the cop cars with Mike Post's catchy music are used as punctuation marks to break up the close up concentration on the drama of the confrontations between the various characters.

16. *To keep this white man off you ...*

This is a high shot of car 60, Hill and Renko's car; they are called out on a domestic. A black woman with a knife, a younger half-naked woman cowers. William, her husband, is hiding in the bedroom. He has been sleeping with the young girl. Hill calms the situation, with great skill and tact. He presents Renko as this bad white cop he is only just keeping in check. The wife gives up her knife and Hill lays down the law for future conduct in the family. He leaves them with a variation of Esterhaus's catchphrase, 'You take care now ...'.

27. *A brand new unit, second one today ...*

Hill and Renko exit the run-down building. Their car has been stolen. Renko yells saying he'll get it back if he has to shoot up the street. Hill tries to calm him as curious and threatening characters gather. All the pay phones are vandalized, so they enter a building looking for a phone. They surprise drug dealers who shoot them. (37:50)

> By now we have grown to appreciate the way Hill and Renko work together. We are in their story point of view (*see* later chapters). We see the dynamic of their relationship and the creative way they use their respective racial identities. We are starting to feel affection for them, the way we do for series' characters. Then, in a terrific coup de théâtre, they are shot. Are we being manipulated? Yes. Does it work? Yes.

18. *Throw something out the door ...*

Furillo's car arrives as helicopters gather overhead. He tells the cops to holster their weapons as he tries to talk to the hostage-takers through a loud hailer. He asks Hector to throw something out. Hector throws out a toilet roll – the crowd laugh. At the back of the building, the heavily armed EAT team muster fitting explosives to the door. Hunter smiles as his helicopters shake the building. The noise makes it impossible for Furillo to negotiate.

19. *Just take those helicopters out of there ...*
    Inside, as the hostages cower and the teenager holding a gun on them gets more and more nervous, the building vibrates. A bottle falls off a shelf and crashes to the floor. The EAT team think this is a gun going off. They blow the door, burst in and shoot up the shop. Furillo, furious, throws himself over Hector and the other kid to protect them. Hunter has got his way.

    > The action climax of the siege is dramatic and slightly farcical. It is a miracle that no one gets hurt. The net effect of it is to set up the characters of Furillo and Hunter. Furillo is brave and terminally liberal, prepared to risk his life for the most disadvantaged criminals of the ghetto. Hunter is dangerously stubborn, his approach nearly leads to a bloodbath but his self-satisfaction is also comic. From the writers' point of view, this is money in the bank for future episodes.

20. *Go home Frank ...*
    Joyce Davenport arrives at the station. Of course there is no suspect, La Rue comes on to her. She pours her coffee on his crutch. His partner laughs, 'Your place or mine'. (44:22)

21. *We can't raise Belker ...*
    Esterhaus tells Frank that they can't raise Hill or Renko on their radio. Belker and Lamonica are sent to find them. Phil tells Furillo to go home. Frank says he will.

22. *Fascistic uncaring animals ...*
    In a darkened flat, Joyce Davenport is in a bathrobe with her long hair in a turban. She is haranguing someone we can't see, while cleaning her teeth. She says the outrageous behaviour of the police amounts to police harassment. When we see who is in her bed, it is Furillo. She climbs on the bed and kisses him.

    > We get the climax of the La Rue/Davenport subplot. We see the affection, tempered with disapproval for his foolhardy methods, that Esterhaus and Gomez have for Frank. Then we get another twist when we find that Frank and Joyce are lovers and all the time we know something they don't, namely that Hill and Renko are probably dead. The personal is always upfront but the dangerous background, the violence of the cops' ghetto beat, perpetually threatens to engulf their lives with tragedy.

23. *Night exterior.*
    Belker and Lamonica pull up before the derelict building. They go in and find the bodies of Hill and Renko.

24. *Your pants are buzzing.*
    In the flat, Furillo and Davenport have made love. Furillo's pager goes off. He makes the call and learns that the wounded Hill and Renko are in intensive care. (48)

We are left with a cliff-hanger for next week's episode and with most of our major characters introduced. We have seen them in action, in danger, in love and in the fall-out of divorce. The two writers, Michael Kozoll and Steven Bochco, and the director Robert Butler have done this in barely 49 minutes.

Exercise
- Watch *Hill Street Blues* with this breakdown. Examine how the world of the story, the themes and the characters are introduced.
- Now watch a much later episode and see how those have developed.
- Choose another contrasting TV pilot and, using the above as a model, make your own step outline.
- Examine how the writers approach the world of the story, the themes and the characters.

THE PRECINCT AS FAMILY

When you examine any precinct drama, you find that whatever the precinct (and in this context hospitals or East End squares are also precincts), the characters seem to form a sort of family. Indeed you could argue that American TV drama of the last five years was all about various kinds of dysfunctional family from *The Sopranos* to *Six Feet Under*. In *Hill Street Blues*, detective Furillo is a sort of father, Esterhaus a sort of uncle or even a mother, and the cops their unruly children. These traits, while it does not do to labour them, are partly to do with the domestic way we consume TV. The days of families clustering around a TV to watch together are largely gone, but I know several families who do not even eat together, and yet gather to watch *The Simpsons*.

Because we allow TV drama into our homes, we require it to reflect the home environment. The most exact demonstration of this was in *The Royle Family* (UK 1998), Caroline Aherne's groundbreaking comedy (*see* Chapter 10). In this show, she made the dominant camera position the TV set itself and the subject the family watching it. The camera seldom moved and never left the house. This often painful focus made the sofa became the precinct, and the unflinching gaze revealed a wealth of often heart-breaking comedy.

The precinct is, of course, the world of the story and how well you know this world, and how economically and instantly recognizably you create it, will largely determine the success of your drama. Successful TV drama creates a kinship, even an ownership, of the drama in the audience and this impacts on the writer. He must find in his plots strong emotional, even familial, threads that will bind the audience to him over many weeks and months, and people them with characters that, because he loves them, we will grow to love or love to hate.

Checklist
- What is your precinct or main location?
- What is your plot?
- How well do you know it?
- What research do you need to do?

THEME

When considering a pilot episode it is useful to consider the theme. Let's examine a very different kind of police drama, this time from the UK.

Prime Suspect by Lynda La Plante

The first episode of *Prime Suspect* was a single story lasting 203 minutes. It created a running character played by Helen Mirren who was to appear in six other similar length TV films. On one level it is a standard police procedural; that is, a drama that follows authentically the steps of a police investigation. Linda La Plante is an expert at getting this right, but this for her, unlike many other writers, is only the beginning.

In *Prime Suspect*, a Detective Chief Inspector takes over when a colleague dies and duels with a clever serial killer, George Marlowe (John Bowe), in order to find the evidence to convict him. However, the theme of the story lies in DI Jane Tennison's frustration at her lack of promotion, particularly in the last eighteen months when, although eminently qualified to lead the Murder Squad, she has repeatedly been passed over. Indeed, she has spent her whole career banging her head against the glass ceiling, contending with the institutional chauvinism of the police force. Jane Tennison has to fight on three fronts: trying to resolve her relationship with her partner Peter Rawlins (Tom Wilkinson) and her squad of officers, led by the destructively hostile Sergeant Bill Ottley (Tom Bell), but also to solve the crime. The genius of La Plante is that all three are given equal value, and where a lesser writer would have allowed the feminist theme to overwhelm the police story or vice versa, each strand is enriched by the other. *Prime Suspect* should be in every serious TV writer's DVD collection but it is only necessary to analyse one sequence to give the flavour of how the investigation works with and against the theme of how women are regarded in the home and the workplace. Here then are the beats that I mentioned earlier, and you can use this as another example of how to work with a step outline.

It is 56 minutes in and things are going very badly for DI Jane Tennison ...

George Marlowe is to be released.

Tennison announces in the incident room that they must release George Marlowe, they don't have enough evidence. They protest and Otley takes a call.

I knew you'd get me off.

Exterior in the rain, Marlowe and his lawyer leave. Marlowe, asks his taxi to wait and goes to Tennison in her car. She winds down the window, he says – I knew you'd get me off. She winds up window and on the other side Otley tells her another body has been discovered.

> In a fine piece of direction by Chris Menaul, Jane is shown in her car sandwiched between the murderer and her hostile colleague. Otley's car on one side, Marlowe at the window of Jane's car. The theme of chauvinism and the battle of wits between Jane and the murderer is made concrete.

We knew we had the right man.

They visit the scene of the crime. Tennison falls in the mud and Otley ignores her. The officer in charge will only talk to Otley. Jane insists on seeing the victim's face and identifies her as Della Mornay. Ottley rubs in the fact that Tennison released Marlowe, who has probably done this one too. The two male coppers exchange looks.

Why is there never a pencil?

Working late, Tennison breaks a pencil; searching for another she finds Della Mornay's file inside Otley's desk. She also finds the prostitute's diary with pages torn out. A light goes on and a cleaner bursts in. In her own office she examines the diary and the missing pages. Her mac, draped over a radiator, catches fire.

> Again, she is working later and longer than her male colleagues. The only other person there is the female cleaner, who works round her, as she makes the chance discovery that will allow her to turn the tables on them. The point is not laboured but it is naturally present in the simple action of the cleaner turning on the light.

I hardly ever see you.

In bed at home, exhausted, she is woken by a kiss by her lover Peter, who has just got his son back to sleep. He complains that she is ignoring him. She starts to make love to him but they are interrupted by the little boy.

> The theme of the collapse of her private life is dramatized with humour and tenderness. She is trying to keep all the balls in the air but somehow ...

Off the record ...

The next day she gives the squeamish young copper a lift to the Morgue. There she persuades the pathologist to say that, off the record, he thinks it's the same murderer.

I'd like him to stay.

In her boss's office with Otley, it seems as if Detective Chief Inspector Kernan is about to take her off the case. He asks Otley to leave. Tennison insists he stays. She produces Della Mornay's file and asks why Della was initially wrongly identified when she was well known to both Shefford and Otley. Otley tries to bluster, saying that she is just getting at a dead man. She produces the diary. This is evidence that has not been either bagged nor logged. Kernan tries to reassert authority but Jane has won. She uses this success to get costly round-the-clock surveillance of Marlowe and also to take charge of the press releases from now on.

She let you off.

She leaves, Kernan makes Otley hand over the pages he has torn out and tells him, 'She let you off, I won't'.

> Her use of this triumph, not to destroy Otley but to gain more resources for the investigation, illustrates how she has a more subtle and intelligent approach than her male colleagues.

Your drama may have an obvious theme but it should arise naturally from the actions of the characters. If it seems that scenes are only there to illustrate the theme, you will lose your audience.

> It's corrupting to write with the intent to moralize, to elevate people's moral standards.
>
> Susan Sontag, *Diaries*.

Women struggling with the institutional chauvinism of the police force is a good theme. It is one that Linda La Plante was made well aware of, from talking to the few senior female police officers in the UK. Indeed, she could have extrapolated it from the role of the female writer/producer in television. However, had this theme been all she had, the story would not have worked. What works so well in *Prime Suspect* is that the demands of the thriller form are so well served: suspense, tension and surprise are all provided. The details of the police procedure are never fudged. Indeed the action, as with *Hill Street Blues*, is anchored in well observed and researched police detail. The theme emerges from the action, not the other way around.

Checklist
Questions to ask yourself:

- Does my story have a theme?
- What is it?
- Does it at any moment seem to overwhelm the plot?
- Are there scenes that seem just to illustrate the theme rather than drive the plot along?

4 CHARACTER

WHAT MAKES A GOOD TV CHARACTER?

> ### Protagonist
>
> Protagonist comes from the Greek *protos* (first) *agonistes* (actor/combatant). So your protagonists are the people whose actions drive your story. The choice of this word, rather than the more passive word 'character', is significant. It suggests action, struggle ... even a fight.

In a single drama the central protagonist, the hero, drives the plot forward by his or her actions, or sometimes by the things that are done to him. Within the limited compass of a feature film, about two hours, we know that our protagonist will struggle, fail, triumph but in some way resolve his or her difficulties before the credits roll and the lights come up. We also subconsciously know that we will not see this character again. Let's leave aside the question of sequels because, although these are made, they are seldom made unless the first film is successful. Their impact on the plot and character is generally limited to action heroes not being killed off in the last reel, just in case they should need to come back.

TV characters are not circumscribed in this way. The episode ends and, if we like the character, we leave the room and make a cup of tea and think, 'I'd like to see them next week'. Again, we are back to the domestic nature of TV consumption. Because we want characters to return, we want them to be, however uncomfortable their lives, in some way comfortingly familiar – like a worn overcoat. Indeed, one of the best-loved TV characters could be said to have been defined by his worn overcoat or his mac – Colombo. If we think back we see Ironside with his wheelchair, Maigret with his pipe and Inspector Morse with his crosswords and his beer. The same technique was used to define the members of a vaudeville act like the Crazy Gang or the Marx brothers. Each character had his instantly recognizable attributes.

Harpo Marx

Harpo Marx so successfully played being dumb that many believed he truly was. The story goes that his father was watching the brothers one night when the man next to him in the theatre said of Harpo, 'That boy's been dumb since birth'. The father, without revealing who he was, said he didn't think so. 'Bet you ten dollars that boy is dumb', said the stranger authoritatively. Father Marx looked at the stage and famously didn't take the bet.

We become so used to the characters they play, that it is often a shock to see them in real life. I remember at an early age, on work-experience at Granada TV, meeting the cast of *Coronation Street*. As I brought them their cups of tea, I was almost shocked at how smart, out of costume, they were. Now intellectually I knew that they were not the Northern working-class characters they were playing, but their roles were so engrained in my imagination that this group of well-paid and quite theatrical actors, gossiping about the profession, seemed an odd betrayal of the well-loved characters. We feel not only that we know long-running TV characters but also that we own them. Part of the writer's job is to foster this feeling. The current celebrity culture has extended this and now soap stars are almost expected to have a private life as publicly interesting as the characters they play. '*EastEnders* Phil in punch-up' – not for a moment does anybody feel the need to expand that headline into: actor who plays Phil in punch-up. He is, of course, called Steve McFadden.

Historically, how much of the enjoyment of series like *Maigret*, *Columbo* or *Morse* was due, not so much to the plot, as to watching the character work. We want to spend time with these people even if, in reality, we would find Columbo's mac repulsive, Maigret's pipe smelly and Morse's shrewd but curmudgeonly bachelorhood tedious. Characteristics that make our protagonist instantly recognizable might not at first glance be ones that are attractive. They often become attractive through repetition and also through the charisma of the actor who plays them. In TV, the more you study it, the more you find that the kind of characters audiences warm to can be described as 'flawed saints'. Those who strive to do good but often, inadvertently, do bad. Also, even when they solve crimes or heal people, they do so at great cost to themselves. There is no better 'flawed saint' than Jimmy McGovern's *Cracker* (UK 1993) and its less successful American re-incarnation (USA 1997).

INTRODUCING A CHARACTER

In Episode One, *The Mad Woman in the Attic*, Jimmy McGovern introduces Dr Eddie 'Fitz' Fizgerald in close up on the phone. He is listening to the commentary on a horse race, while a nervous and impatient man waits behind him. Fitz is urging on his horse, which loses. The waiting man turns out to be an academic. Fitz is about to give a lecture. The academic introduces him and Fitz, after a glance at the apathetic students, hurls volumes of philosophy and psychology into the audience – 'Spinoza, Descartes, Hobbes, Locke, Freud ...'. He hurls the last book and says, 'End of lecture' and walks out of frame. He comes back in, 'Moral?'.

We then cut to the train, where the conductor discovers the murder victim. She will turn out to be an ex-student of Fitz.

We cut back to the lecture, where Dr Fitzgerald is saying, 'The bride in white, sees herself as the widow in black ... . I rehearsed the death of my own father for years ... so lock yourselves away for a couple of days and study what is here. [He strikes his chest.] The things that you really feel, not all that crap that you are supposed to feel. And when you've shed a little light on the dark recesses of your soul that is the time to pick up a book.'

Jimmy McGovern's writing is shot through with a strong sense of Catholic guilt. We are all sinners. Fitz is no clean-limbed caped crusader. He has all the vices. He embraces them. He smokes, he drinks, he gambles, he tries to borrow money off his children. He is thoughtless and cruel to his wife. Yet these very sins are also his work method. He solves the case by empathy. He is one of the fallen too. Later in the story, we see that the detectives interrogate the suspect from a position of moral superiority but Fitz puts himself in the position of the criminal. He even claims he is worse, because he doesn't act out his horrific fantasies. The 'bride in white' speech is a credo. Unless you know yourself, how can you know others. Fitz is a wonderful fallen saint. He has nearly reached rock bottom and yet he offers to help the grief-stricken parents of the murdered girl. The portrait is unflinching and unsentimental and it places the conflicts within the main character up front. It is a fine piece of writing and is hugely entertaining because it doesn't, unlike Fitz, hedge its bets. We love him because he is not trying to win our love. Fitz's conflicts drive the story as much as the investigation of the student's death.

CASTING

You may argue that the writer has no control over who plays his character, but this is not true. Sometimes that control is exercised in a roundabout way through the quality of their writing.

> Ever since I said Robbie Coltrane couldn't possibly do Fitz – I have had nothing to do with casting ... . I have learnt over 25 years that casting is a great skill and I haven't got it. I have ideas and they are so obvious and I have ideas that are so wrong and I kick against ideas which in retrospect, in hindsight, are absolutely wonderful – the casting of Robbie Coltrane ... .
>
> Jimmy McGovern interviewed by Mark Lawson BBC Radio, 28 July 2006

Of course *The Mad Woman in the Attic* benefits from a superb cast, excellent direction and production (Michael Winterbottom and Gub Neal, respectively). Of course the casting of Robbie Coltrane, one of the few comedians who can act, is an enormous bonus, but what drew him to the role? It was Jimmy McGovern's writing. When an actor reads a part, he or she is looking for emotional and physical characteristics that he can work with. It is often said that actors would rather play villains than heroes because the villains get all the best lines.

Actors can't make bricks without straw and they can smell powerful writing through a brick wall. This episode is a classic. Download the script of this episode and read it. Then hire the DVD and watch it; you will learn a lot.

Like Fitz, the character you create must not just simply function as detective, doctor or lover. He or she must drive the plot along but must also suffer in that world of the story. The all-knowing detective who has no weak points is charmless. The healer who does not need to be healed is un-involving.

Six Feet Under

In the pilot episode of Alan Ball's *Six Feet Under*, it is instructive to look at the introduction of Nate Fisher and Brenda Chernowith, I will be returning to how this relationship is developed by the writer in later chapters.

> If the Fishers are imagined by Strindberg or Ibsen, the Chenowiths are a family imagined by Sophocles.
>
> Alan Ball

The series begins with Nathaniel Fisher, Nate's father, being killed by a bus, just after he has had a conversation with his wife Ruth about how cancer will kill him if he doesn't stop smoking. Ruth's concern is cleverly intercut with Nathaniel's smoking and careless driving. She hangs up. Taking advantage of her complaining about a friend of hers who has had to put up with her husband running off with a man, David, her gay son, looks as if he will seize the moment to come out of the closet, but he funks it.

Nate and Brenda come through the arrival gates at LAX. Nate, attracted to Brenda, gives her his phone number. He remarks that he was expecting his father to meet him. Brenda says she can give him a ride, he declines; she says, 'I wasn't talking about that kind of ride'.

There is an exterior of the funeral home and then David is talking with a client. His phone rings and he has an argument with Claire, the Fisher's teenage daughter, about attending the family Christmas.

A closed door at the airport with the sign 'Authorized Personnel Only'; inside the broom closet Brenda and Nate screwing. Nate says something endearing and Brenda says, 'Shut up and fuck me'.

Cut to the turkey coming out of the oven. Ruth is told of Nathaniel's death. She hurls the turkey and other things around the room. David downstairs hears this, he comes up. Ruth tells him, 'The new hearse is totalled and your father is dead'.

We go back to the lovers kissing in the broom closet. The dialogue goes like this:

> BRENDA
> Just so you know, I don't do this.
>
> NATE
> Me neither. Will you at least give me your name.
>
> BRENDA
> Probably not.
>
> NATE
> Why?
>
> BRENDA
> Because I'm a realist.

Nate's cell phone rings and his brother David tells him of his father's death.

We learn an enormous amount about all the characters from this sequence. As regards Nate and Brenda, we learn that she is impulsive, perhaps promiscuous, that both she and Nate are driven by very strong desire and, indeed, a certain love of danger. That Brenda has few expectations of relationships but that Nate seems to want something more than the sex. The whole atmosphere and the linking of love, both in the sexual sense and in the interlocking patterns of caring between the Fishers, also shows us love always in the context of death.

Brenda, because she is so intimately 'with Nate' when he hears of his father's death, is tied to him in a very special way. Had it not happened, the pair might have straightened their clothes and slipped out of the broom closet and gone on their way. The news of Nathaniel's death ties them inevitably together.

Jimmy McGovern and Alan Ball are very different writers. Culturally and geographically they could not be further apart, but they both present their characters without flinching. Showing us their good and bad qualities, without a moral spin but with a strong belief in their reality. It is clear that they love these characters.

Look at the way these writers introduce and develop their characters, but as with all analysis it should not lead to mere synthesis! Good writers do not strive to make their characters more interesting, like cooks frantically adding spices. Good writers, as I said in Chapter 1, observe the way people are. They show the world through the eyes of those characters; this is story point of view.

Nobody is two-dimensional in life and none of us thinks of ourselves as two-dimensional. Creating a paper-thin character is as much a failure of empathy as of observation. Unless you love your characters and allow them to take you over, then you will never create people who walk and talk like real people. This is also true in the group-writing situation where you often have to fight for your character. A dialogue in the writer's 'room' might go like this:

> 'My character wouldn't do that.'
>
> 'Why not?'
>
> 'Well ... she just wouldn't.'
>
> 'That's not an answer. It is possible.'
>
> 'Just ...'
>
> 'Well, what if she did?'

This kind of testing also takes place when you write on your own but of course the voices are all your own and the 'room' is in your head. It is important to test your characters and not to let them become complacent. Of course in soap writing the necessity to raise the ante often creates just this kind of artificiality, when a character has to be hyped-up for melodramatic effect. This seems perfectly legitimate, given the nature of the genre. Part of the attraction of writing for soaps is how far you can push these boundaries without losing your audience. To quibble at this would be like objecting to the Victorian villain twiddling his moustaches or the heroine shrieking as she is tied to the rail tracks.

Exercise

As well as watching the above episodes, watch *ER* and think, in the context of the healer who needs to be healed, about Nurse Abby Lockhart (Maureen Tierney) in *ER*. Compare and contrast with Dr Gregory House (Hugh Laurie) in *House*.

Checklist

Behaviour – what does your character do when challenged?

- What/who do they love?
- What do they do with their love?
- Do you know them?
- What do other people in the story think of them?
- Do they inspire trust?
- Is what you see what you get? Are they transparent or devious?
- What are their strengths and insecurities?

5 Dialogue

I worked with Renee Goddard at the European Script Fund and she had witnessed the growth of TV drama in Britain during the 1950s and 1960s. I was fascinated to hear her recall that when writers for TV asked how much they might be paid for their work, they were told by the powers that-be that they would be receiving less than they did for radio drama, as the images were being supplied without their help.

Christian Routh, Pilot's workshop, 1994

As I said in Chapter 1, TV drama is the love-child of radio and theatre and this still impacts on the way writers write for TV. The first TV dramas were live, and with great ingenuity the action would move around the various sets in the studio to be picked up by the multiple cameras. Writers and directors would have to work to create scenes that flowed with some of the continuity of a live theatre-piece. If you watch a classic early TV drama like *1984*, the ingenuity is dazzling and though some aspects of the acting style may have dated, it is instructive to compare the flow of the dialogue with a show like *The West Wing* (NBC 1999–2006), which although not shot live, echoes this tradition.

In cinema films, the dialogue can be sparse because the film will rely for its effect on short scenes, shot out of sequence and edited later. The power of a film can often be, not from the words but, from an individually lit close-up, a combination of the actor's expression and the cinematographer's skill. Lacking the twenty-foot wide screen, few TV dramas, although they are often composed more or less entirely of close-ups, end with anything like the look in Garbo's eyes in *Queen Christina* (1933) that seems to sum up her tragedy.

At the end of the film, after she has abdicated as Queen and she is exiled from Sweden, Don Antonio dies in her arms. Christina stands as a silent figurehead at the bow of the ship, the wind blowing through her hair. The camera tracks in on the blank enigmatic expression on her face, what was she thinking at the time? Director Rouben Mamoulian told her to think about 'nothing ... absolutely nothing ... . I want your face to be a blank sheet of paper. I want the writing to be done by everyone in the audience'.

Generations of movie-goers have done just that, written their emotions about the film onto the twenty-foot close-up. Whatever alchemy this is, it is not TV.

THE STEADICAM

Increasingly the steadicam, a counter-weighted camera that allows the cameraman to follow the actor with ease, without the necessity of laying tracks (rails for the camera to run on), has created a fluid style that has begun to dominate TV.

The cameraman follows or leads the actor from room to room. A character will leave 'taking' the camera with them and when she leaves the shot, another actor will 'take the camera' with them like passing the baton in a relay race. This allows writers to have bravura pieces of dialogue spoken on the move with characters handing on their ownership of the camera. If you watch any episode of *The West Wing*, you can see this technique in action. Often whole scenes are accomplished without cuts – in the USA these are called 'one-ers'. TV likes them because they save time and therefore money.

TV drama can often provide the space for dialogue sequences to stretch out in a way that the cinema cannot.

In the cinema, the words can be just an adjunct to the image. In TV, where for example you may have a permanent set that holds few visual surprises for the viewer, they often have to carry the whole weight of the drama. In a radio play, dialogue has to make us 'see' the Oval Office, the casualty ward or the squad room. In TV we can see these places but then we saw them last week and the week before, and their very familiarity makes them almost disappear, giving us a unique focus on what the characters actually say to each other. As cinema has gone more towards spectacle, TV has in some ways become more theatrical. The ability of camera and actor to be linked umbilically, to dance together to defeat traditional montage, has often made the dynamics of dialogue drive the action.

HOW TO WRITE GOOD DIALOGUE

To write good dialogue you must be able to hear your characters speaking. The most common fault is for writers to write all their dialogue in their own voice. There is a simple test for this. Set out your dialogue in stage play format.

> CHERYL: Roger you cheated me!
> ROGER: I know I'm a heel.
> CHERYL: Why do you always lie?
> JULIET: (Enters) What is it with you two?
> CHERYL: Bitch!

Then lay a ruler across the characters' names. Do Cheryl, Roger and Juliet all speak with the same voice? If they do, this is bad dialogue.

Van Gogh's Ear for Dialogue
A cheap joke but some writers do seem to be tone deaf to dialogue, while others have a natural ear. In the same way, some people just do sing in tune, while

others cannot distinguish between two notes. These lucky writers find dialogue easy. Because they can hear their characters in their head, the dialogue flows naturally, but even these lucky ones sometimes come across characters that they can't hear. Perhaps they are from a background or region that is unfamiliar to them.

How to Train Your Ear

For this we must go back to the disciplined observation that we talked about in Chapter 1. When people speak, listen, but listen critically. What does this person's delivery tell me about them? Is he affecting his machine gun/100 words a minute style or is this really the way he thinks. Does she drawl her words for seductive effect or just because it takes her brain a bit of time to get her ideas straight. Most people speak in a way that reflects their personality or, as in the case of Tony Blair, in a way that reflects the way they wish to be perceived. A study of his speech patterns would reveal a chameleon-like ability to adapt his accent to suit the audience he is addressing. This is very common in the UK where the patterns of speech still tell you so much about the class system and the status of people. So toffs speak in pretend cockney or 'mockney' and a motorist will consciously pitch his voice up a class when caught speeding. Although the tortuous ramifications of the British class system that lead to Tony Blair's occasional forays into Estuary English, a flat uninflected 'classless' accent redolent of London's Thames Estuary, all over the world people will speak in a different way in a different situation.

When you are with members of your family, you speak differently from the way you do in the office. Schoolchildren speak among themselves, not only with a different tone to the way they do with their teachers, but also often with a different vocabulary. The writer must train himself to listen and reproduce the way people speak in different situations, just as he must train himself to really look at what people wear and how they move.

A Simple Exercise

Take four of your friends or work colleagues and try to write down examples of the way they speak. When you are confident that you have done this well, put the four characters into a simple situation, say arguing over a bill. Write this dialogue, then get somebody to read it to you. Can you hear your friends' voices?

VERNACULAR AND ARGOT

Before you start to write for a show, you should consider two things: vernacular and argot.

Vernacular (n) One's mother tongue.

Every series has its vernacular, this may be the regional speech of *Coronation Street* or the languid upper-class drawl of *Brideshead Revisited*. But as a general rule there will be a way that the characters in a series speak.

In the following dialogue from Alan Bleasdale's *The Boys from The Blackstuff* (BBC 1982), the scouse accent fixes the characters in Liverpool but it is not just the accent, it is the whole rhythm of the dialogue – this is their vernacular.

The Boys are eating breakfast in a caff before starting the day's tarmacking. They are all on the dole, so it is illegal work. Yosser has persuaded Dixie to ask for more money. Dixie, anxious not to rock the boat and possibly lose this precious work, has reluctantly done this.

> DIXIE
> Oh yeah no sweat – nother fiver for youse.

> CHRISSIE
> (snatching back bacon from Loggo.) Where's me sodding bacon gone?

> YOSSER
> Oh we'll know next time.

> CHRISSIE
> You don't want to push it Yosser we're on a good enough screw as it is.

> YOSSER
> It'll be even better when the jobs unionised.

> DIXIE
> You can't stop you. You never know when to leave well enough alone....

> YOSSER
> Look dickhead, I've been around. I know the score. I just haven't greased the same boss for the last ten years. I've been down South. Saudi Arabia, Nigeria, The Shetlands...

> LOGGO
> What's it like th' Shetlands?

> YOSSER
> (to Loggo) Cold and full of ponies. (back to Dixie) I've been around.

> DIXIE
> Yeah I know Yosser, you've been everywhere. You're going nowhere now sit down will ya.

> YOSSER
> You like hospital food?

The social climate and the TV climate that produced *The Boys from the Blackstuff* has vanished, yet it remains worth watching as one of the few masterpieces of television. Few writers are so closely anchored in their community as Alan Bleasdale is in Liverpool. He is writing from the heart of what he knows well, something that all writers should strive to do. For the purposes of studying dialogue, the six films of the series are a pitch-perfect example of vernacular. How people speak, relates totally to who they are. The dialogue is by turns terse and baroque; it will flirt with sentimentality only to suddenly ground you with wit and an unflinching ear for reality.

It is of course easier if you were born where your series is set but if you have to write for a show that is set somewhere else, then you must immerse yourself totally in the vernacular of this world. You must become like a spy in another country. You must make the language of the series become your mother tongue.

Argot (n) Slang, that of thieves and vagabonds.

Often a show will also have its argot. I use this originally French word for a very precise reason. Thieves develop slang to define their tribe and also to stop other people finding out what they are talking about. In, say, *CSI* the characters often resort to their private language.

We as outsiders may not understand this forensic jargon but it creates a mystery that defines the world of the story. The well-groomed lab rats of *CSI*, like the Parisian thieves, use a private language to show they belong and define their trade. We may not understand what they are talking about but it makes them seem authentic. Of course in the workplace characters don't always talk about work. They may talk in the argot of their leisure activities, which again throws their characters into sharper definition. Here is an example of this in a scene from the pilot of *CSI* Written by Anthony E. Zuiker.

Scene 08:
INT. CSI – HALLWAY – NIGHT
 NICK takes the 'SOLVED' magnet off of the whiteboard and puts it directly in his column: 'NICK' over the block: CRIME 99 'UNIDENTIFIED PERSON'. The other blocks in his list include: 100: ASSAULT; 98: DRUNK DRIVING; 97: RAPE; 96: ASSAULT. NICK punches the SOLVED magnet proudly with his fist. He smiles.

NICK STOKES
(Under his breath.) One more, baby, one more.

NICK stares at the board proudly. WARRICK turns the corner and puts a hand on NICK'S shoulders. He turns to look at the board, too.

51

> WARRICK BROWN
Hey.

> NICK STOKES
There he is. What's up?

WARRICK takes the 'SOLVED' magnet off of the whiteboard and puts it directly in his column: 'WARRICK' over the block: CRIME #99: ASSAULT.The other block in his list includes: #100: ASSAULT and #98: ROBBERY.

> WARRICK BROWN
Ninety-nine. You and me, dead heat. Next crime solved gets promoted to CSI-3, man.

> NICK STOKES
Yeah, yeah, choice of shift, $8,000 raise, extra week vacation-oh-ho, it's all about Cabo, bro.

> WARRICK BROWN
Twenty bucks, by the end of shift, I'm the man.

> NICK STOKES
Is there anything you won't bet on?

> WARRICK BROWN
Nah. It's college football season, man. I won eight of ten this weekend.

Nick and Warrick are betting on their crime-solving abilities. As the discussion moves to betting on football, the argot of the practised gambler takes over. Even if this is incomprehensible, it draws us into the relationship of the two characters and enriches our view of their world.

> WARRICK BROWN
(continues) Kilt 'em. Outside the Huskers and them punk-ass Irish, I'm up about four G's.

> NICK STOKES
Hmm, what's the line on us?

> WARRICK BROWN
On us? I'm like tiger, man – I'm heavily favored.

> NICK STOKES
Come on, give me a winner for tomorrow.

> WARRICK BROWN
(sighs) Ah... green bay, minus seven and a half over niners. Always go with the better quarterback.

> NICK STOKES
Uh-huh. Cool.

WARRICK walks past NICK.

                    NICK STOKES
Hey, good luck tonight, man.

NICK holds out his hand and they shake hands.

                    WARRICK BROWN
Thanks. You, too, Nick. I hope you get that trick
and roll. You'll never crack that in a shift, never.

WARRICK walks away.

                    NICK STOKES
(to his retreating back.) Yeah, well, we'll see, and
I hope the pack wins by seven.

The writer has to maintain a balancing act between authenticity and mystifying the audience. The use of argot has to be sparing and judicious. The jargon words have to be built into the rhythm of your characters' speech, otherwise it can become pretentious or just plain incomprehensible. You must always be aware that those who use jargon in the workplace are often unaware that they are doing it. They do not always use it to baffle outsiders, sometimes it's just the way they speak. Also, audiences are smart, they pick up on the argot quickly. Pretty soon the writers do not need to hold up the story by translating, 'Can I have that in English please?'. Indeed, relishing the argot becomes a part of enjoying the series.

So as well as the vernacular of a series, you will have to learn the argot of a series. Often argot is used in a medical series to set the scene and put us instantly in the world of the story. Here is a good example from *House*, a show where the central character often delivers tongue-twisting, high-velocity medical jargon. But here we see the argot folded in to the vernacular, as the characters – all of course doctors – discuss the patient.

INT HOSPITAL CORRIDOR
(Walking)
                    DR HAMILTON
The enzyme protocols working, reversing the ALS.

                    DR FOREMAN
The timing doesn't seem suspicious to you?

                    DR HAMILTON
Do you think Dr House will see it that way? Figure
it's his medication doing the job.

                    DR FOREMAN
I'm sure he will.

INT HOUSE'S OFFICE
                    HOUSE
(reading file) It's one of ours see.

> DR ALLISON CAMERON
> How do we figure out which drug is doing the trick?

> HOUSE
> Easy we stop all of them.

> DR ALLISON CAMERON
> One of those drugs is helping him.

> HOUSE
> And the rest? Steroids, anti-biotics,
> anti-inflammatories – their toxics.

> DR ALISON CAMERON
> He'll walk again.

> HOUSE
> Yes, to his own funeral.

> DR ROBERT CHASE
> But if we stop everything. He'll get worse.

> HOUSE
> True but then we'll add our medications back one at a
> time. Then, if he gets better, we'll have our answer.

> DR CAMERON
> And if he doesn't?

> HOUSE
> Then we're in trouble, not as much as he is …

We may not understand what the two doctors in the corridor are talking about but they set up the dramatic effect of House's bold plan to save the patient. In this scene there are drug names but they are not unfamiliar. They anchor the dialogue in the world of medicine but do not keep us out. We may not know what antibiotics are but we've all taken them and so we move from the exclusiveness of the first doctor's dialogue in the corridor to the inclusiveness of the scene in House's office.

Doctor and Patient

In the pilot episode of *The Sopranos* (written and directed by David Chase), Mob Boss Tony Soprano (James Gandolfini) has collapsed at a family barbecue. The medical tests have proved there is nothing physically wrong. His doctor has suggested he consult a psychiatrist. Reluctantly he has agreed to do this and the action of the first episode is framed within the sparring dialogues between him and his therapist Dr Jennifer Melfi (Lorraine Bracco). In these conversations there is the conflict of two argots – two private languages – psychotherapy and the Mob; much of the entertainment is in the collision of two ways of speaking. These ways of speaking are also of course ways of seeing the world. Their first meeting goes like this.

                    MELFI
My understanding from your family physician,
Dr Cusamano, is you collapsed? Were unable to
breathe? Possibly a panic attack?

                    TONY
They said it was a panic attack – because all the
neurological work and blood came back negative.
They sent me here.

                    MELFI
You don't agree you had a panic attack?

He laughs too loud.

                    MELFI
(cont.) How are you feeling now?

                    TONY
Now? Fine. I'm back at work.

                    MELFI
What line of work are you in?

                    TONY
Waste management consultant.

Tony Soprano's whole life is about deflecting questions,
about lying. Melfi's is all about eliciting the truth –
indeed most of her dialogue is questions. Things
progress to where, after a certain amount of bravado, he
begins to admit that he is depressed. The ducks referred
to are a family of ducks who had their ducklings on
Tony's pool and then flew away, significantly on the
morning of the day he collapsed.

                    TONY
Dysfunction this! Dysfunction that! Dysfunction
va fan cul'!

                    MELFI
You have strong feelings about this.

                    TONY
Let me tell you something – I understand Freud.
I had a semester and a half of college. So, sure,
I get therapy as a concept. But in my world it doesn't
go down.

He stares at her.

> TONY
>
> (cont.) Could I be a little happier? Sure. Who couldn't?

> MELFI
>
> Do you feel depressed?

He averts his eyes. Admits.

> TONY
>
> Since the ducks left, I guess.

> MELFI
>
> The ducks that preceded your losing consciousness.
> Let's talk about them.

He simply gets up and leaves.

In Tony's world, you must never show weakness because if you do, then your status could be fatally compromised. The job of the psychotherapist is to let him admit his vulnerability. So the cat and mouse game continues, as often as not when Melfi touches a nerve, Tony's only response is to get angry or leave. Melfi prescribes him Prozac, he feels better.

> MELFI
>
> It's not the Prozac.

> TONY
>
> Why not?

> MELFI
>
> You said you were thinking clearer and your wife
> told you you seemed better. It's not the medication.
> Prozac takes several weeks to build up effective
> levels in the blood.

> TONY
>
> (disappointed) What is it then?

> MELFI
>
> Coming here – talking. Hope comes in many forms.

> TONY
>
> Who's got the time for it?!

She maintains that maddening shrink stare.

> MELFI
>
> What is it you really want to say to me?

Tony Soprano is used to fixing problems, quickly and often with violence. In psychotherapy there are no quick solutions, so there is always this tension between Tony wanting a quick solution and Jennifer who, knowing this is not possible, being in it for the long haul.

As their relationship develops, Melfi's questions and determination not to rise to Tony's aggressive behaviour begins to wear him down, so that he starts asking questions of her and even begins to cry over the ducks.

> TONY
>
> You're right – that's what I'm full of dread about, that I'm going to lose my family. Just like I lost those ducks. It's always with me …

> MELFI
>
> What are you afraid is going to happen?

> TONY
>
> (completely rattled.) I don't know! But something. I don't know!

Tony Soprano, by submitting to psychoanalysis, puts himself into a world where they literally do not speak his language. Here all the things that define him, and one part of that is his argot, the private mob language, are of no use. The dynamic of the scenes is often created by this mixture. The textures like the colour of oil and water swirling together in a muddy puddle. The richness of the language reflects the constant push and pull of morality in the series. The struggle between the two kinds of family values that Tony's life represents, on the one hand his care of his wife and children and on the other his obligations and status within the Mob.

You can learn much from studying these scenes and indeed much of the dialogue in *The Sopranos*. Notice how one character will push while another pulls. Notice how characters in their dialogue do not always match noise with more noise. Notice how the language of nurture, ducks, school-age children, mixes with the bloody language of dealing with stool-pigeons and debtors.

What a character says may not always be true, but the way he or she says it is.

Questions About Dialogue
- What is the argot of my character?
- What is the vernacular of my series? (In *The Sopranos* Italian American, in *The Black Stuff* Scouse.)
- Do my characters understand each other?
- If they don't, what efforts do they make to speak each other's language?

6 STRUCTURE

THE TV HOUR

In Chapter 1, I listed various formats. Obviously the structure of what you write will be dictated by the slot you have to fill. In TV it is generally very important to write to time. You also need to know whether your drama is to be broken up by commercial breaks or not. It is much better for the writer to build these in rather than leave them to chance. In the BBC, or in a subscription channel like HBO, you do not have to contend with the high-volume interruption and inevitably inappropriate advertisers' messages. In a series like *Spooks* (BBC) the 'TV hour' is a full 59 minutes; in *24*, where the hour is broken up with commercials, it is only 42 minutes. The TV hour structure is generally four acts and sometimes a coda or tag.

In this chapter, as we come to them, I will define and explain various key words, buzz words of scripturgical literature that you will come across. These are: coda, dynamics, character arc, turning point, climax and denouement.

CODA

> **Coda**
>
> In music, a passage after the natural completion of a movement.
> So as to form a more satisfactory conclusion.
>
> OED

Because episodic drama should always leave you wanting more, it is fitting to start with defining a coda. The coda exploits the feeling we mentioned above that you want the show to continue. Time has passed since the climax and denouement, about which more later, and the coda adds an essential grace note to the episode. It suggests for good or ill the future lives of the characters. In American TV, the coda is called the 'tag' – it could be described as the future in the glow of the past.

See below for an analysis of the TV hour; this four-act shape, I would maintain, is the basic building block of TV drama. It is generally best to think of a two-hour show, a pilot say, as being composed of two of these blocks.

DYNAMICS

Dynamics

Dynamics is the science of the action of force in producing or changing motion.

The cue ball smacks into the spot ball and sends it spinning across the table. It cannons off a stripe ball and sends both balls in different directions. This is the action of force in producing or changing motion.

What makes a plot move is some kind of force against which your character must struggle. Our heroine is imprisoned, so she must break out; she does so and the plot begins. If characters do not have anything to fight against, there is no plot.

In a sitcom this struggle can be with a car that doesn't start, as with Basil Fawlty (John Cleese in *Gourmet Night*, episode 5 of *Fawlty Towers*) or in high drama, as when Jack Bauer (Kiefer Sutherland in series two of *24*) races to prevent terrorists planning to explode a nuclear bomb in the middle of Los Angeles.

Dynamics is also a musical term and it refers to another kind of movement, the movement from soft to loud and back again. It is often useful to think of the disposition of your plot – when things happen – in terms of music. Is this bit loud? Is this bit soft? Or equally usefully, Is this sequence dark? Is this sequence light?

A plot that doesn't have this dynamic is dull. So when we consider structure, it should always be with an eye to dynamics. To organize the events according to some blueprint is not enough. You must organize them so that conflict keeps the plot in motion. These conflicts may not all be epic, they can often be quite small things. They can be comic, as with Basil and the car, or potentially tragic – Jack and the unexploded bomb.

CHARACTER ARC

Character Arc

The path of a character's emotional or moral journey through a story.

In a feature film, the arc of the character dominates structure. How and when things happen to a character, the actions that a character takes to overcome the obstacles thrown at him or her, create 'the turning points'. The turning points in a plot are when a character suffers or does something that changes the direction of his life. It is the smack, as the pool balls cannon, spin off the cushion or crash satisfyingly into the pocket.

TURNING POINTS

> ### Turning Points
>
> Those moments in a story when characters are confronted by choices, actions or insights, which significantly affect their character path.

In a feature film or a single drama, the various turning points create a sort of graph of the character's fortune – the highs and lows of their story. This moves towards a climactic confrontation of some sort when the story is resolved. If this graph flat-lines, that is has no turning points, then the story will be very boring and the audience are likely to feel cheated.

In a single movie, we are with a character for two hours and his/her adventures, the varied turning points, are the spine of the plot. A good example of this is in Chapter 3 (*see* pages 39– 41) when I discuss the turning points in *Prime Suspect*. The path Jane Tennison describes in this is a roller-coaster ride of ups and downs. But in an episodic drama, the more significant character arc can occur over many episodes. For example, in a show about a forensic pathologist, the heroine might lose her husband in episode 3. This informs how she feels over episodes 6, 7 and so on. Of course the hero of a detective show can have little or no character arc. Detective Columbo in 69 episodes and Ironside in 198 hardly changed at all. There were turning points in their investigations, but the weekly solving of the crime and capture of the criminal had little or no effect on their character. A stalwart of British TV's Sunday night viewing is Agatha Christie's Hercule Poirot. The celebrated Belgian detective has been incarnated by many actors but to my knowledge has never had a significant turning point or indeed a character arc. His personality remains as fixed as his waxed moustache.

THE TV HOUR

Let us imagine a one-hour TV drama episode and use it to examine the shape of the TV hour. These act breaks will often, but not always, correspond to the commercial breaks. The page numbers for one-minute pages are for a 58-minute hour but of course if the hour you are writing for is shorter, then each act will have fewer pages.

When I write a TV hour, I turn the A4 page on its side and set out five columns. In these I list the various incidents roughly where they come in the story. If you make your columns in ink and your incidents in pencil it is easy to change them. At a glance you can see how long you've got to get to the second murder! You can do this electronically if you prefer.

It would look something like this.

Act 1 (1-15 pp approximately)	Act 2 (15 pp approx)	Act 3 (15 pp approx)	Act 4 (12 pp approx)	Coda or Tag (5pp approx)
MEET HERO	HERO LOSES CLUE.		HERO FINDS NEW CLUE	FATHER AND DAUGHTER BOND.
THE THREAT	DAUGHTER KIDNAPPED	LEWD THREATS TO DAUGHTER		
MEET DAUGHTER	BOMBER DISCOVERS POLICE HAVE BEEN INFORMED.			
		POLICE STING GOES	LAST MINUTE RESCUE	
SMALL BUILDING BLOWS	ERO RECEIVES HIS DAUGHTER'S SHOE.DEADLINE MOVED BACK!		BOMBER LED AWAY	

Act 1 (15pp. Approximately)

The Set Up. Our hero has a problem. A madman is threatening to blow up a building somewhere in the city unless he receives an unfeasibly large sum of money by 4.00 pm. Our hero has to find him. Since there is generally a secondary problem for the hero, let's say his daughter has not returned home from school. The act ends with the bomber blowing up a small building to show he is serious.

ACT 2 (15pp. Approximately)

Things get worse. Our hero loses the only clue he has. He learns his daughter has been kidnapped by allies of the bomber. The bomber, discovering that the police have been informed, says they now only have till 3.00 pm to come up with the money. Our hero is sent his daughter's shoe to persuade him to give up.

Act 3 (15pp. Approximately)

... and worse. The allies of the bomber are now threatening to perform lewd and unmentionable acts upon his daughter. A police sting goes badly wrong due to them not listening to our hero.

Act 4 (12pp. Approximately)

In the nick of time our hero finds a new clue that has been staring him in face all along. He gets the bomber and saves his daughter and her honour. The bomber is lead away in chains.

Coda or Tag (5pp. Approximately)

A relieved father and daughter bond, they even joke about their lucky escape.

Expressed as a diagram our hero's path in a TV hour looks as shown in the diagram on page 64.

TV Two-Hour Structure

Let's now expand our bomber story into a TV movie. Perhaps a potential pilot for later hour-long episodes. We now have seven columns and we are still talking one-minute pages. Using the breakdown below, make your own diagram of the hero's fortunes. Think about how you can create climaxes and mini-climaxes to make the graph more of a switch-back ride.

Act 1 (13–16pp. Approximately)

Our hero, divorced, looking after his daughter, somewhat of a maverick in the police force and so on. His life is complicated by his ex/late wife and by a boss who insists on playing by the rules. As he juggles bringing up the wayward daughter, with appeasing his boss, the bomber strikes and ominously his daughter does not return home from school on time.

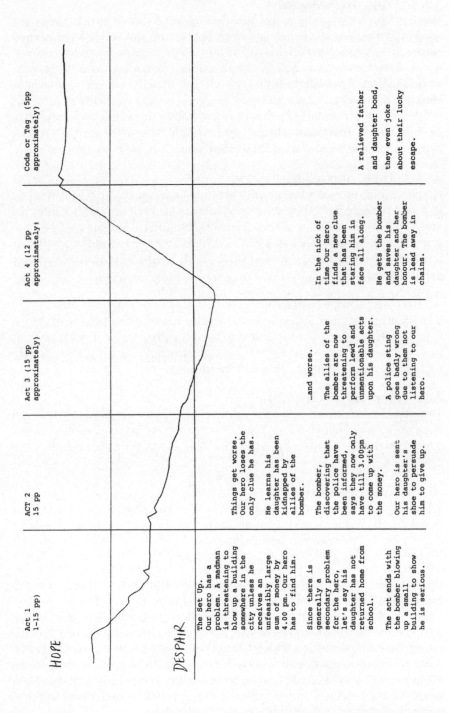

HOPE

DESPAIR

Act 1 (1-15 pp)	ACT 2 15 pp	Act 3 (15 pp approximately)	Act 4 (12 pp approximately)	Coda or Tag (5pp approximately)
The Set Up. Our hero has a problem. A madman is threatening to blow up a building somewhere in the city unless he receives an unfeasibly large sum of money by 4.00 pm. Our hero has to find him.	Things get worse. Our hero loses the only clue he has.		In the nick of time Our Hero finds a new clue that has been staring him in face all along.	A relieved father and daughter bond, they even joke about their lucky escape.
Since there is generally a secondary problem for the hero, let's say his daughter has not returned home from school.	He learns his daughter has been kidnapped by allies of the bomber.	...and worse. The allies of the bomber are now threatening to perform lewd and unmentionable acts upon his daughter.	He gets the bomber and saves his daughter and her honour. The bomber is lead away in chains.	
The act ends with the bomber blowing up a small building to show he is serious.	The bomber, discovering that the police have been informed, says they now only have till 3.00pm to come up with the money.	A police sting goes badly wrong due to them not listening to our hero.		
	Our hero is sent his daughter's shoe to persuade him to give up.			

63

Act 2 (10pp. Approximately)

News of the kidnapping of his daughter and increased threats from the bomber. A blood-stained shoe is sent to Police HQ. The bomber blows up a small building to reinforce his point.

ACT 3 (10pp. Approximately)

His boss, still sticking to the rulebook, suggests a sting involving staking out the delivery of some marked notes. Our hero knows this won't work but has to go along with it. In a major crisis he is proved right. The police are made to look like fools and the bomber shortens the deadline.

ACT 4 (10pp. Approximately)

His boss seems more concerned with blaming someone else for the fiasco and so saving his own neck than solving the crime. Our hero has lost his only clue and there is an ominous silence from his daughter's kidnapers. Our hero storms out into a rainy city as if just by dejectedly tramping the empty streets he might solve the case. He howls into the dark. When he is at his lowest ebb, his mobile rings.

ACT 5 (10pp. Approximately)

Somehow his daughter has sent him a message. He returns to HQ, armed with this clue. He confronts his boss, having taken the precaution of going over his head first, his boss must now play it his way. But the bomber calls, his daughter is being punished for sending him the message.

ACT 6 (5pp. Approximately)

Time has almost run out, while the police forces muster, our hero slips in to the back of the building where the bomber is hiding. He watches as the bomber sets up the radio control for the bomb. The bad guys prepare their getaway. The clock ticks.

ACT 7 (5pp. Approximately)

The spectacular police assault (helicopters, SWAT back up, etc.) begins but our hero from the inside disables the radio control of the bomb and, as the bomber tries to use his daughter as a human shield, he tops him. A chastened boss leads the mopping-up operation, while father and daughter are reunited.

In this longer structure there can be a more leisurely set up. There is time to establish the characters with more detail and even to provide a back-story. Those good at maths will have noticed that I said the two-hour drama was composed of two one-hour blocks, that is four acts, but the two-hour TV movie schema has only seven acts. This is because the first act is a set up act and obviously you don't need to have another set up act if the story is continuous. What you will get if a drama is spread over two days (evenings) is that day two generally starts with a sort of pre-trailer that briefly summarizes the highlights of yesterday's or last week's episode – 'the story so far …'.

This is very schematic and the plots are derivative and banal. More imaginative writing often shifts these act breaks but I am inclined to think that, when writing for broadcast TV, these acts are rather more useful than the Hollywood three-act structure is for feature films. This is simply because shows are broadcast in 'slots' and these 'slots' are made up of TV hours. This, of course, may change in the years to come when we are consuming TV in a dialled-up stream, rather than according to the TV guide. We are all aware of how different the experience is of watching a series on DVD rather than week by week. Writers will be as affected by this as is the audience.

Exercise

Make your own diagram of a TV show you admire, using the diagrams as models. Note where the various beats, the climaxes and reversals, come in relation to the TV hour.

THE SERIES

In a series, the shape of the hour will have previously been dictated by the storyliner. How exactly the story is hammered out, whether it is in the writing room, where the writer/producers gather, or outlined in a more authoritarian way by one story creator, will vary but you will have to work with its plot.

> How a story is assigned to one of the core group of writers is often determined simply by who's available at the time, or who expresses an affinity for a particular story. On occasion, when none of the writer/producers have the time to write a script, the story will be assigned to an outside writer. But no matter who writes an episode, they are all based strictly on the outline that's been given them.
>
> David Chase creator of *The Sopranos*

Not all shows are as well-structured and 'policed' as *The Sopranos* but inevitably any show, to have coherence over a number of episodes, and of course in the USA they have many more episodes than we do here, must have a strong controlling structure. The danger of this is what I call, 'whiteboard plotting' where the desire to tick dramatic boxes overtakes the creative element leading to drama by numbers.

So how do you use that structure creatively? My suggestion would be that, rather than mechanically trying to hit your climaxes at certain page numbers, regard it much more like glancing at a clock when you are swimming. It helps to know where you are in the hour. What the characters do must be authentic and lively but their stage is that hour and they must act within it. To create good scenes that tell a story, even if it is not your story, is a real skill and it is not a small thing to do. You are also helped in episodic drama by the fact that your characters have a history; you can use this either by following it or by playing against its predictability – the 'this character wouldn't do that' factor.

A genuinely surprising action from a character can often give him or her a new lease of life.

Climax

From the Greek for a ladder – the highest point of the action. The peak of the drama.

The climax is not necessarily the end of the show. It is when the conflicts generated by the protagonists reach a final crisis of confrontation either physical or emotional. What is certain about any kind of climax, be it action or psychological/emotional, is that it generates energy. It is the skill with which you use that energy that creates a satisfactory ending.

DENOUEMENT

Dénouement

Dénouement is the unravelling of a plot or story; the issue event or outcome. From the French *dénouer* to untie.

If you imagine the plot as a rope of tension stretched to breaking point and snapped at the climax, then what you are left with is a tangle of broken strands. Sorting out the threads of the plot is the dénouement. The most obvious example of this is in detective stories where after the climax (e.g. the gun being wrestled from the killer's hand), the detective untangles the threads of the plot both for the other characters in the piece and also for us – the audience. Of course in a romantic comedy the untangling of emotional threads replaces this. A lot of comedy comes from actually creating such a tangle.

TV MOVIES

TV movies are often thought of as the poor relation of cinema films. Indeed, one of the favourite phrases used by film producers to reject a feature film script is, 'I think this would be more suitable for TV'. This is almost unanswerable as nobody really knows what a TV movie is. It is not just a question of scale, since small-scale films like *The Full Monty* have had cinema success. Nor is it a question of the basic inferiority of the form, since directors of the calibre of Robert Altman and Stephen Frears have returned to TV after making successful feature films. Indeed Frears's *My Beautiful Launderette* began its life as a TV film and only went on to have a successful run in the cinema almost by accident. An acknowledged masterpiece like Kieslowski's *A Short Film about Killing* formed part of his TV mini-series *Dekalog* (The Ten Commandments,

1987). The definition has to be – any film financed and primarily intended to be shown on TV. Though more and more of these are now made with, at least the hope, that they may get some kind of cinematic exposure. This of course generates very useful publicity. Column inches and exposure at festivals, all increase the buzz about a film, even if they don't generate any box office. There are many admirable TV films from Peter Watkin's *The War Game* to Steven Spielberg's taut debut, *Duel*. Often the short schedules and constraints of TV, its limitations, lead directors to find creative solutions.

> With TV movies, either you run them or they run you.
>
> Steven Spielberg

It can also be argued that unruly talents like Ken Russell are disciplined to do their greatest work on TV, though personally I find this a rather simplistic evaluation of Russell's work. There are also many examples of fine TV directors who appear to lose their talents when they hit the big screen.

TV movies are still hugely popular in Europe, particularly Germany, but are becoming something of a rarity in the UK. Original TV movies, that is fictions created specifically for TV rather than adaptations and factions, which were once the glory of UK TV, are now as rare as hen's teeth. Perhaps uniquely, Stephen Poliakoff has kept making these. Here is what he says about TV films as opposed to cinema films: 'I do have two [cinema] films in development. But with television, I have total artistic control. My work reaches a great number of people and that's better than having a film out for two weeks and then it disappearing.'

So what demands does the TV movie make on a writer? Well again we are back to the TV hour or rather two of them yoked together. In all probability, unless he or she is writing his movie for a cable channel or the BBC, he will have to be aware that it may be broken up into TV acts. The budgetary constraints may be balanced by a greater artistic freedom, but against this there will be censorship and broadcast guidelines. If it is a network show, certain words and actions may be forbidden. I was shown a note from CBS in the 1980s which said, 'No off screen groping'; a slightly difficult one to work out that. As regards structure, over the seven acts the fortunes of a pair of lovers in a two-hour TV movie is shown in the diagram opposite.

You can make up your own love story and then draw the switch-back ride of the character's emotions.

THE PATH OF TRUE LOVE

> We spent all season two condemning Brenda and all season three redeeming her.
>
> Alan Ball (*Six Feet Under*)

HOPE

DESPAIR

Act 1 (15 pages approx)	Act II 10-10c pages	ACT III [10-11 pages)	ACT IV [10-11 pages	ACT V (15 [10-11 pages	ACT VI (8- [5-7 pages	ACT VII) [5-7 pages
Two lovers meet instantly attracted they make love.	Circumstances force them apart and he fails to act decisively	They meet by chance and it looks as if he will finally declare his love but at the last moment he loses his nerve.	Filled with remorse they both pine but eventually decide to get on with their lives.	The woman marries another and The Man despairing proposes to an old flame they are to be married.	On the eve of the wedding the Man learns that the Woman is now free but he feels duty bound to go through with the marriage.	However in the final moments he backs out of the wedding and amid much chaos pursues his true love eventually they are finally united.

In a subtly written series like *Six Feet Under*, a character can go through changes both within the episode and over many episodes and seasons. In the first seven episodes of season one of *Six Feet Under* (the full season was thirteen hour-long episodes), we see a far more complex and unresolved love story. Nate and Brenda come together fuelled by great sex! They are pulled apart sometimes by their own wilfulness but also by their exceedingly complex familial loyalties and back-story. I suggest you get the DVD for Series I.

Here are the significant turning points in Nate and Brenda's relationship in just the first seven episodes of *Six Feet Under*. The beats are marked in bold so you can follow them with the DVD. The selections of dialogue are to help you navigate.

Episode 1: The Pilot
1. Nate and Brenda meet and screw in broom closet at airport.

Episode 2: The Will
Their relationship blossoms.

2. Nate discovers that Brenda has 'Nathaniel' tattooed on her back.
Nate: You must have loved him to have his name burned into your flesh.
Brenda: I'd have done a lot more than that for him.

3. Catharsis on the bus.
Brenda helps both Nate and his brother David come to grips with their grief by taking them on the bus that killed their father.

Episode 3: The Foot
Brenda and Nate have sex.
Brenda: You make the weirdest noise.
The unspoken question over this episode is: is Nate going back to Seattle?
Nate: You are my woman.
Brenda: I love that look.
They drink champagne Brenda has stolen from her mother.
Brenda buys Nate a concert ticket for three weeks away.

4. Brenda magicks with the future.
Nate: How did you know I'd still be here?
Brenda: I didn't.

5. Brenda magicks with the past.
They have sex in the deserted house, now bought by the Fishers' rivals Kroehner. Nate dreams of his childhood.
Brenda: I'm glad you are staying in town.
The deserted house burns down.

Episode 4: Familia
The police question Nate and Brenda about the fire.
Brenda comes to supper with the Fishers.

6. Ruth catches Nate going down on Brenda and drops a vase.

After the uneasy dinner party, Brenda says Ruth hates her. Sex doesn't solve everything.

Brenda brings an apologetic gift for Ruth who tells her:

7. Be careful of Nate, he's a lot more fragile than he looks ... .

The question that hangs in the air is, did Brenda start the fire for Nate?

Episode 5: An Open Book

Nate meets the Chenoweths (Brenda's parents). He has dinner with them alone! Learns of *Nathaniel and Isabelle*, a children's book that obsessed Brenda, when she was growing up. This is the 'Nathaniel' tattooed on her back. Nate and Brenda row.

8. Trust undermined. Nate turns on Brenda: Why do you mind fuck me?

Should I trust you? Nate is introduced to the book *Charlotte, Light and Dark*, the book about Brenda by her manipulative psychiatrist parents. Nate dreams of Brenda as a little girl. He finds the key to his father's secret room. David comes out to his brother.

9. Trust further undermined. Nate meets a naked Billy, Brenda's brother, in Brenda's flat.

He has the matching Isabelle tattoo on his back.

Ruth: You really don't believe in God?

10. Brenda: No. Sometimes I wake up so fucking empty I wish I'd never been born. But she says it in such a way that it could be a bitter joke.

Episode 6: The Room

At breakfast Nate is so totally absorbed in *Charlotte, Light and Dark* that he doesn't listen to Brenda, always a bad idea. Flashback to Brenda as a child saying her doll has been raped.

Brenda: I'm leaving, do you still want a ride?

Brenda gets close to Claire, tells her that as a child she barked like a dog for a month. Claire says this is so cool. Flashback to this. Nate and Brenda in Nate's father's secret room.

11. Brenda nails Nate: You didn't know [your father] when he was alive. You can't know him when he's dead.

Brenda smokes dope with Claire.

Episode 7: Brotherhood

Nate sleeps in his clothes.

Brenda: Your life stinks. You need to take a break.

Nate: Oh God I love you.

They plan to go away together.

12. Their fucking is interrupted by Billy. Billy's agenda; is this chance?

Brenda comes to dinner again. Claire talks of the Sierra project. Nate reveals he went on this project as a child too. He leaves with Brenda. They find gifts from Billy for their weekend – chocolate, wine and a dildo. When Nate looks askance, Brenda says: Don't judge him please. Billy has crisis while choosing photos, so Nate and Brenda can't go on the weekend. Nate protests.

13. Moment of choice – Brenda chooses Billy not Nate
Brenda: You think I fuck my brother?
Nate: I never said that.

14. Brenda: Just go goddammit.

The various turning points mapped above, as they discover both each other and each other's families, complicate their affair over the extended storyline and the longer time frame. By the end of season two, Nate and Brenda's projected marriage has, in a total of 26 hours of screen time, been scuppered by Brenda sleeping with strangers. Her fear of commitment seems to have destroyed their love. But of course there is season three so the redemption Alan Ball talks about, which could not have been dreamed of in a single drama, is possible. Two people who, however conflicted, seem to be made for each other, may in future seasons be re-united. Love, over the next seasons, may triumph but I won't tell you if it does. You will have to watch season three. However there are three other love stories in the first season they are:

- Ruth and Hiram
- David and Keith
- Claire and Gabe.

With various degrees of intensity, they have similar switch-back emotional paths. If you were to take coloured pencils and obsessively map them all in the same way I have mapped the above, you would end up with something like a Jackson Pollock. Its very abstraction would show you how this kind of schematic analysis only goes so far. Use the DVD of season one to look at the relationship of Nate and Brenda, and see how it impacts on the lives and loves of the other characters in the series. This kind of complexity developing over many weeks (episodes) is unique to TV and can create a depth of character only otherwise found in novels.

The geographer of this complex character path, and the keeper of the bible of a series, is the storyliner, the person who keeps control of the series' plot. If hired to write an episode, you will have to write your episodes with his or her road map in mind.

It is important to treat the bible not as a limitation but as a chance to release your inhibitions. There will be plenty of people prepared to pull you up. The story creator, script editor or producer will all have their say. Research the bible and really get to know the characters. The better you know them, the more inventive they can be. Writers are hired for their individual talent, not for their subservience. Even having your ideas shot down can be stimulating. Here is a young writer talking about the experience of working with Paul Abbot on the ground-breaking UK series *Shameless*.

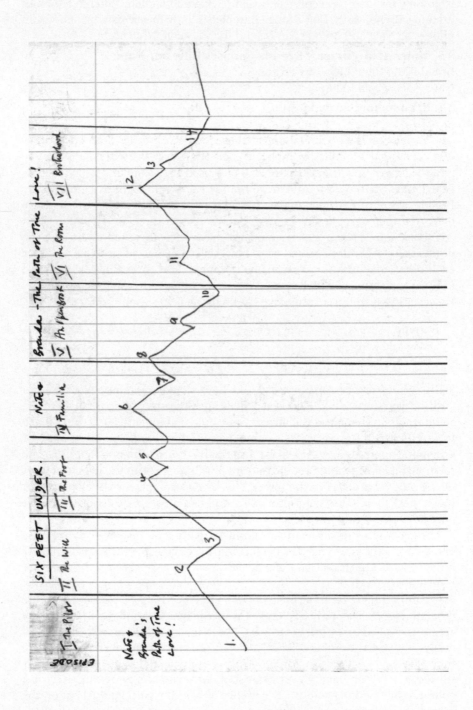

> I loved working with Paul Abbot. He encouraged me no end, never rubbishing an idea, just coming up with a better one. It was a bit of a crazy schedule trying to fit in round all his many commitments and pressures, but I've never met anyone so generous with his time and ideas ...
>
> Phil Nodding (*Scriptwriter Magazine*, Issue 27)

A writer secure in his or her talent is more often than not likely to be helpful like this. It is the producer or script editor whose grip is slipping who will cause you problems.

HALF-HOUR EPISODIC TV STRUCTURE

Leaving aside soaps, a half-hour TV drama is generally a comedy. There is really only time for two acts, with a prologue/set up and perhaps a coda; interestingly this shape corresponds to Aristotle's 'quantitative parts of comedy':

* prologue
* choral part
* episode
* exit.

The following is US writer/producer Jason Brett's analysis of a traditional American sitcom, a vintage episode of the Lucille Ball show, *I Love Lucy*. I have taken the liberty of laying it out in columns. He is talking about one-and-a-half minute pages. He makes the point that the writer's first draft varies in length according to the show.

This classic TV sitcom shape is useful as a template against which to examine sitcoms. It is surprising how often even modern shows still fit it.

I will be returning to comedy later (Chapter 10) but it is useful to note that, in comedy, nobody ever learns from their mistakes. In *Men Behaving Badly* (1990) the men behave badly next week in exactly the same way they behaved badly this week – nobody learns anything. The dynamics of Gary, Tony, Dorothy and Deborah are as fixed a dance as that of Lucy and Ricky and the Mertzes (*I Love Lucy* 1951). In more than forty years, sitcom characters have learned nothing!

A half hour drama on the other hand is like a short story in two acts. Within the short compass of the form a problem is set up, complicated and then resolved, either comically or tragically. The characters do have some development but because of the clock (*see* Chapter 7), you have to use great economy.

Before we leave this chapter, let us put our buzz words in chronological order – story order if you like. The dynamics of the plot create turning points for the character whose character arc develops as he or she moves from climax, through denouement to the end coda. One word is missing from this litany and it is 'finale'.

Teaser (1-3 pages)

Typically, witty banter and jokes that put the characters into their relationships and environment. (Does not necessarily relate to the episode's story)

ACT 1 (15 – 20 pp)

Sets up the problem(s) or "hook": establishes who the episode's major character is, and their problem.

"Lucy wants to audition for the amateur talent show at the club, but Ricky won't let her."

Set up subplot.

"Lucy and Ethel audition in disguise, and get into the show."

End with complication, cliff-hanger or act break.

"Rickey and Fred find out what their wives have done, and decide to play along and let the wives make fools of themselves."

ACT 11 (15-25 pp)

The "Block Scene" – a seven minute, extended set piece of physical or behavioural comedy where things go from bad to worse for the lead character(s)

"Lucy and Ethel perform and everything that can go wrong does – including Ricky finding out."

Tag (1-3 pages)

Like the teaser, this may or may not relate to the story. Typically, it's a moral or a big laugh.

"Lucy learns her lesson…but finds out there's going to be another amateur show and conspires with Ethel to try again…)

> **Finale**
>
> From the Latin *finalis* meaning the end, this is the last movement in a musical, the concluding number of an opera. The whole cast is assembled on stage singing their lungs out.

In series drama, for obvious reasons, you seldom get finales. The exception is at the end of a season. A good example might be *The Grand Opening*, the final restaurant scene in series three of *Curb Your Enthusiasm*. In this the chef, who suffers from Tourette syndrome, unleashes a symphony of swear words. In order to spare chef's embarrassment, Larry swears too and gradually everybody in the restaurant, very much in the manner of the ensemble in a grand opera, joins in a glorious finale of filth.

Exercise
- Using the diagrams, examine an hour-long episode of a series and see if you can spot the act breaks, the mini-climaxes and so on.
- Think about the four-act structure.
- Watch a TV movie and see how, when you put these two hours together, 4 + 4 = 7.
- See how, with the longer format, the set up is more detailed.
- Lastly, look at a favourite half-hour comedy and ask yourself, does it still seem like two acts, with a prologue and a coda? Can you spot the ghost of *I Love Lucy*?

7 TV Time

In any drama there are always two times to consider: the time of the action and the time of the audience watching that action. We have looked at the domestic way TV is consumed and the way this makes it make different demands on the time of the audience to a play or a film. Shall I watch this week? Shall I bother to watch next week? Increasingly viewers are time-shifting, using devices like Sky Plus and TiVo to manage their viewing habits. They are also not waiting till next week to see next week's episode but jumping over to the digital channel (More 4, ITV 2, BBC 4) from the terrestrial channel. DVD release is almost instantaneous and people often have long sittings watching a whole series – *Soprano* evenings, *Six Feet Under* afternoons or *Sunset Beach* weekends! This is a kind of gorging, like eating the whole box of chocolates, but it goes some way to creating an event out of the essentially passive activity of watching TV.

The uncertainty as to how and in what frame of mind your audience will be watching will continue to change as technology advances. Because of this uncertainty it is vital that the writer has a strong grip on the time frame of his drama, what I call the clock of the drama. If you as a writer don't have this, then you cannot hope your audience will stay with you after they have gone to check on the meatballs and spaghetti.

The Clock

The Three Unities

The three classical unities are rules for drama derived from Aristotle's Poetics. In their neoclassical form they are as follows:

1. The unity of action: a play should have one main action that it follows, with no or few subplots.
2. The unity of place: a play should cover a single physical space and should not attempt to compress geography, nor should the stage represent more than one place.
3. The unity of time: the action in a play should take place over no more than 24 hours.

The clock of any drama starts at the beginning of the story and ends at the end. In classic Greek drama, the clock of the drama – the time that the story covered – was identical to the clock of the audience. If action in the play took place over two hours, then the play was two hours long. This classically simple idea was exploited famously in the film *High Noon* (directed by Fred Zinnemann, screenplay by Carl Foreman from a story by John W. Cunningham). This film lasts 85 minutes and the action of the film also lasts 85 minutes. The audience is living the same amount of time as the characters. This simple device gives great tension and continuity to the drama. This very old idea was brilliantly used by the series *24*, which I will examine later in this chapter. Time-based devices, like flashbacks and voice-overs, often stop the hurtling clock of any drama; in TV this is often further complicated by the commercial break.

STORY POINT OF VIEW

Story Point of View (SPOV)

SPOV is not to be confused with the instruction POV (point of view) that you will find in a script (*see* Chapter One and Glossary where the camera is 'seeing' with a character's or even an animal's eyes. It is sometimes called subjective camera. We all know the werewolf's POV: the camera rushes low, brushing the grass aside, as the panting werewolf slavers towards its prey. That's POV.

In general, our attitude to the clock of a story is conditioned by who tells the story or whose story it is, SPOV. The emotions of the main character affect the speed of the clock if you like. Time for the slacker is not the same as time for the man trying to save the world.

In *24* the ticking clock always belongs to the Counter Terrorist Unit agent Jack Bauer. Even when we move away from him to scenes where he is not present, the events always relate to his situation. When you are writing a drama, you must always consider from whose point of view the story is being told, as this will have an impact on the clock of the story.

VOICE-OVER

Voice-overs are unrealistic, we do not hear them in life, but we regularly hear them in drama. The simplest is the voice-over that tells us what a character is thinking. If you are writing one of these it is always a good idea to think of the images that accompany the words. If the voice-over draws you away from the clock of the story, you must make sure that it brings you back, having learnt something important. It is all too easy for a voice-over, particularly when adapting a novel, to be the lazy option. Voice-over should never describe things that you are seeing anyway or emotions that you could show with action.

Some good examples of the use of voice-over would be in *Sex and the City* (HBO 1998–2004) and in complete contrast *The Street* (BBC 2006). Voice-over is often used to tell us about back-story.

BACK-STORY

The back-story consists of the events that happened before your story begins – it precedes the clock of the story. It is often essential to know the back-story to understand the present story. But mere narration of the back-story takes us away from the clock of the story – the headlong rush of events. It can relax the thread of tension and so the writer must be clever in the way he presents it.

If we take the episode of *The Sopranos, College*, we can see how the relation of the back-story is folded into the tension of the present tense narrative. To re-cap: Tony Soprano is taking his daughter Meadow to check out prospective colleges for her. He spots a middle-aged man filling his car with gas and gives chase. Meadow is puzzled and alarmed by this. The trip has brought a new intimacy between father and daughter but suddenly Tony seems evasive.

We are told the back-story of Febby Petrulio – the man at the gas station – through Tony's snatched pay-phone conversations with Christopher made all the more difficult and dramatic by the rain. These are further complicated by trying to avoid being spotted by a now suspicious Meadow. She catches sight of him on the pay phone and she asks, 'What's wrong with the phone in your room?'.

So we are told the information but always in an atmosphere of tension.

> TONY
> He went on the program. Then they kicked him out.
> Till last year this cocksucker was still flown to trials
> to testify about historical relationships ... he picks up
> speaking fees at college talking about when he was
> a big bad mafiusu.

The present clock of the story is kept ticking as we go into the past clock of the stool-pigeon's history. There is a further level to the back-story in that Meadow's suspicions lead her to question her father closely. He, caught on the back foot because of the stress of killing Petrulio, reveals stuff about his own past that he has previously kept from his daughter.

> TONY
> Look, I put food on the table. (beat) My father was
> in it [the mafia]. My uncle. Maybe I was too lazy to
> think for myself. I considered myself a rebel. But
> maybe being a rebel in my family would be selling
> patio furniture on route 22.

This confidence leads Meadow to tell her father that she and her friends took speed. He gives her some of his history, she gives him some of hers. It is a trade and, because the emotional intensity is kept up, it never becomes just the relation of boring historical facts.

You must always tell your audience about the character's past in the tensions of the character's present. This is a technique as old as the hills. In *Hamlet*, Shakespeare on each occasion when he gives us information about the past, does it within the emotional intensity of the present. The facts of the political situation with Norway are told within the excitement and fear of waiting for the ghost of his father. The facts of his mother's marriage to his father's brother against the tension of a Hamlet dressed in mourning, while the king and his mother are dressed to celebrate their marriage. The information about Hamlet's love for Ophelia is told within the dynamic of her being used as an emotional football by both her brother and her father. So at all times we are getting back-story information in the context of a dynamic present. The clock of the present never stops ticking.

The Fugitive (1963–67) was the most popular TV series of the 1960s. It is consistently voted one of the most popular TV series ever. It has spawned a successful film with Harrison Ford in 1993 and a less successful TV series remake in 2000. It is an immensely durable story.

Doctor Richard Kimble (David Janssen) is wrongly accused of killing his wife. On his way to death row he escapes and spends the next 112 episodes (four seasons – the first three in black and white) essentially trying to discover his true back-story and unmask the real murderer.

The details of the facts of his past he discovers, are always set against the tensions of him trying to hide from the relentless pursuit of the Detective Lieutenant Phillip Gerard (Barry Morse), a character who owes something to Javert in *Les Misérables*; indeed the actor who played him went back to the Victor Hugo novel to get ideas to lend depth to his character.

> I've always thought that we in the arts ... are all 'shoplifters'. Everybody, from Shakespeare onwards and downwards ... . But once you've acknowledged that ... when you set out on a shoplifting expedition, you go always to Cartier's, and never to Woolworths.
>
> Barry Morse who played Gerard

In a sense, any detective story is about discovering and revealing to an audience the real back-story. Writers and the characters they create all have a back-story that enriches the characters in their drama. The community of writers also have a communal back-story: their knowledge and appreciation of all the works of literature and film that have gone before. This, even if we don't actually pillage it, we can all learn from.

Ask yourself these questions:

- What do the audience need to know about the past?
- While giving them this information, do you always maintain the tension of the dramatic present?
- Are you completely clear where, in the time frame of your story, the back-story events are? (A simple chart sometimes helps with this but never put it in the script.)

FLASHBACK

When a writer uses a flashback, he again stops the clock of the story and starts up another clock, the clock of the back-story. If the present of the story is exciting, then we have to be being told something important to be taken away from it. How can we define what this is? How can we be sure that a flashback is justified?

A flashback is only justified if, when you return to the clock of the story, you have learned something vital: Oh, she is his sister; Oh, he is the murderer. In other words, though you have stopped the clock in the present story, when you restart it, you have new information that makes you see things differently. Time has stood still but it has stood still for a reason. You may still be at six o'clock in your story but it is not the same six o'clock. Because of the flashback you know much more, you are in a different emotional place. If you stick to this rule and ask yourself searching questions about the justification of your flashback, then you will avoid those easy and lazy solutions that will alienate the audience. When writing a flashback it is also useful to suggest a different texture for the flashback scenes. This will ultimately be in the hands of the director but it doesn't hurt for the writer to suggest a look or a tone. A flashback could be in black and white or be delineated by music and camera style. A good modern example is *CSI*, where flashbacks are used all the time – literally with flashes. These often dramatic glimpses of what happened at the crime scene or might have happened contrasts with the rather nerdy plod of police forensics. These often horrific incidents are framed by the actions of the glamorous forensic experts and the stylish photography. Here the clock is stopped but because we get new information we do not care. However in *Six Feet Under* there is no change of texture for the flashbacks and they work just as well.

24

This series, created by Joel Surnow and Robert Cochran, brings the classical unity of time up to date and unites it with modern technology. In series one, the hero, Jack Bauer, struggles both to find his kidnapped daughter and to prevent the shooting of a presidential candidate. The mechanics of this drama are totally dependent on twenty-first century technology. It could not have been written before the invention of the mobile phone. The whole 'teckie' armoury is deployed to tell the story – computers, satellite phones, GPS allow the dramatist to traverse the world while sticking to the 24-hour clock. There are 24 episodes of an hour and 24 hours of action. These can even be consumed by the die-hard fan at a single sitting, creating the perfect circle: 24 hours of drama and 24 hours of viewing.

Story Clock = Viewer Clock. Because so much writing for TV is writing to time, it is instructive to look at 24 in some detail. It is a very skilful piece of storytelling and of course it is an illusion. Each episode of 24 doesn't last 60 minutes, it lasts 41 minutes – there are commercial breaks. Both for the dynamic of the story and to allow for these spillages of precious minutes, the writers have to employ a certain amount of sleight of hand. Understanding the skill with which this is done will help you to deal with time in your story telling.

The following takes place between midnight and 1 am on the day of the California Primary.
Events occur in real time.

12 am Permission to transmit.
In Kuala Lumpur local time [4.00.29 on-screen time-check], Malaysia Victor Rovner, an agent, transmits warning of assassination. A shot of a satellite orbiting the earth. In LA, agent Richard Walsh, a high-up officer in the CTU, gets the warning at a swish do.

> There is considerable chutzpah to the way this is set up, because the first visual time-check is not LA time at all but the time in Kuala Lumpur. The shot of the satellite that bridges the nervous agent in the field and Richard Walsh at what looks like an embassy party tells us we are in a world where communication is both global and instantaneous. It sets the tone for linking action in different places in real time, we are all connected always ...

12.01 It sounds like a brunch.
[On-screen time-check.] On the balcony of the hotel, the target of the assassination Senator David Palmer, an African-American running for President, is working on his speech with his aides. A secret service man is seen in the background. His wife enters with coffee, says she can't sleep. They embrace affectionately.

> As the convention of events occurring in real time is established, each sequence has an on-screen time-check, so we know where we are. This scene both establishes Palmer as serious and unpretentious but also a family man. They are all sitting out on the balcony and though the secret service man is there, the politician does not appear to be under threat. We have quickly moved from the global to the personal and, as always in TV, never far from the family.

12.03 I'm glad you moved back in Daddy.
[On-screen time-check] Our hero, Jack Bauer, CTU agent, is introduced at home playing chess with his daughter Kimberly. She is affectionate to her

father but freezes her mother. Jack raids the fridge and, while it's clear that Jack and Terri are putting their troubles behind them, it seems Kimberly is taking it out on mum. The parents agree to present a united front and confront their daughter without delay. Kim however has gone, her window is open. As the parents wonder what to do, Nina Myers, Jack's chief-of-staff, rings. Richard Walsh is coming in to brief them. They are all called in. Jack says he will be back soon. On the move to his car he calls Vincent, an ex-boyfriend of Kim's, of whom he clearly disapproves. Vincent doesn't know where Kim is.

> Jack is introduced, not at work but in the domestic situation. In no more than three minutes we learn that he and Terri have separated, got back together and that their daughter is taking it out on them. Jack is called into the office by Nina Myers and we get our first glimpse of the CTU headquarters and the state of the art communications systems that will allow the mechanics of the story to function. For the audience Jack, at this moment, is a troubled family man with a difficult teenage daughter. He is torn between life and work. By the end of the episode he will be coolly cutting off a dead man's finger to get a print identified but for now, like Senator David Palmer, he's a family man.

12.06 We're hot they'll wait ...
High shot of car, in the foreground a blue clock [visual time-check 12.06]. Kimberly and her friend, Janet York, are going to meet some guys named Rick and Dan at a furniture store. Bauer waits for a bus to pass. It has David Palmer's face on it. This gives him the idea of who the target might be. He rings in to Nina to get him info on this. She asks if he has trouble at home. The teenagers rev up for a party and the slightly odd location suggests that this may not be a good idea. Visually Jack is linked in to thinking about Senator Palmer and because we already know Palmer's the target, Jack's intuitive skills as an agent are established. Nina also seems to be pretty clued up on Jack's personal life.

12.09 It's a different world now Jack.
[On-screen time-check.] Jack on the phone as he walks in to HQ of CTU. Jack says we should remember back when we were teenagers. Terri says will therapy help. He and Terri talk about therapy for daughter. But he is now in HQ and has to hang up.
We like to party ....
Kim and Janet arrive and meet the boys, Rick and Dan. They horse around with them in the furniture store.
Late night news.
[On-screen time-check 12:12:28.] Jack asks ex-colleague on LAPD to keep an eye on his daughter. He is watching the news item, behind the announcer there is a caption saying 'Polls open at 7am'. Richard Walsh enters for briefing.

> All the story elements are now running concurrently. Terri worrying about Kim. Jack putting his personal troubles on hold. The girls partying at the furniture store. The Senator's next public appearance is scheduled and Jack squeezes in concern for Kim between meetings. The story clock and the audience clock are totally synchronous and this unity of time is being exploited to strengthen our empathy for the characters.

Trust no one.
In the briefing we learn that it's a serious threat. A shooter from abroad, who has probably been hired by a hate group. When the others leave, Walsh says there is a traitor in the CTU and he wants Jack to find him. Jack says it's not a good idea for him to do this as his colleagues are suspicious of him. We learn he has just busted three agents for taking bribes. Walsh says Jack is the only one he can trust and urges Jack, in his turn, to trust no one.

> We get a strong sense from this scene that Walsh is someone that Jack holds in very high regard. This respect is mutual and Walsh seems a sort of father figure to Jack. The burden put upon Jack is now increased – can he even trust his own people? In every sequence the pressure on Jack, the problems he must surmount, are ratcheted up as the clock ticks.

When do we land?
At the hotel, Palmer's people get a call from the photographer Martin Belkin who is flying in. They make arrangements. Belkin hangs up and asks the stewardess, When do we land? She replies, that it's twelve twenty and that they land in just over an hour. There is an on-screen time-check.

12:20:08

A beat and then another.

12:22:52

> A few minutes have been lost to the commercial break. The phone call ties this new character to the story. Perhaps Belkin is the assassin? When he asks the stewardess when they will land, this cues a natural time check in her reply, 'It's twelve twenty, in just over an hour'. This reminds us of the time and after the commercial break we are reminded again.

Exercise
- Watch *24*. Hunt for the missing minutes.
- Notice how the writers deal with these, maintaining tension at the breaks.
- Note how clocks and time imagery are used.
- Think about time in your story.

The themes that *24* deals with are not unusual. An assassination attempt, a kidnapped daughter, the tensions in the secret agent's marriage, all these we have seen before. The personal and professional treachery in the workplace (the CTU headquarters must be one of the leakiest high-security operations in fiction) and the buried secret in Senator Palmer's past (did his son kill his daughter's rapist?). The emergence of Sherri Palmer as a bit of a Lady Macbeth, prepared to go to great lengths to safeguard her husband's political career. None of these themes is particularly original but it is in the mixing of these ingredients against the ticking clock that the originality of the series lies.

You will not generally be required to write to time quite so strictly as in *24* but by studying it you will learn a great deal about the techniques of time and story telling: how to manage the clock of the drama and how to use it to create tension.

There is another aspect of narrative time that is unique to TV writing and that is in a series that stretches over many episodes. The audience has a long history of a character. Character arc and the clock of the story can be affected by events that happened many weeks ago. This extended back-story brings us to the subject of the next chapter, which is soaps.

Checklist: Do's and Don'ts of Time-Based Devices

- Is your voice-over really necessary? Never use voice-over as an easy way out either for exposition, character or back-story.
- Suggest in broad strokes the montage. Give the director an idea of the pictures that accompany the voice-over.
- Always be aware that the clock of the drama never stands still. If you return your audience to the same place in the action, make sure that they have learned something significant.
- Are you sure you are not merely avoiding the chore of creating scenes in the present that show the character's past?
- When using flashback, always make clear whose story point of view you are in, who owns the story.
- Suggest a different texture for your flashbacks. Rain against sun, light against dark.
- When constructing a complex drama that moves back and forth between different clocks, make sure that you have worked it out thoroughly by a diagram or a chart. Never put these in the script.
- Story point of view. Make sure that you, the writer, know exactly where you are in the story and whose story it is.

8 SOAPS

It's hard not to believe TV when it's spent so much more time raising us than you Dad.

Lisa to Homer (*The Simpsons*)

THE NEVER-ENDING STORY

There is a story about a journalist going to interview one of the early writers of the still very popular British radio soap *The Archers*. He was proud of his contribution and had a wall covered with shelves of his bound scripts. 'Look' he said to the journalist, 'I've written more words than Shakespeare, mind you I'm not talking necessarily about quality here, but more words'.

There are currently on UK terrestrial TV eleven hours of soap a week. That means in five days you have the equivalent of one whole day or more than a whole evening's viewing. Because of the way they are scheduled, for example, on a Monday you can comfortably switch on Channel Five at 6.00 pm for *Home and Away*, then over to C4 for *Hollyoaks* at 6.30 pm, then on to ITV1 for *Emmerdale* at 7.00 pm, stay with ITV1 for *Coronation Street* at 7.30 pm and then over to BBC1 at 8.00 for *EastEnders*. On Sunday there are omnibus editions of both *EastEnders* and *Hollyoaks*, that allow you to catch up if you have missed anything – a lot of words indeed.

To follow all the soaps is very time-consuming and is really only for full-time couch potatoes, TV critics and those anxious to replace real life with something like real life but more exciting. As someone once said – drama is real life with the boring bits taken out.

In general people seem to be loyal to a maximum of two and are often fiercely territorial when discussing their merits. Like supporters of rival football teams, they are deeply loyal and switching loyalty is a painful process.

Another reason there are a lot of words are that words are cheap. The soaps are generally without expensively staged dramatic incidents and even the few rare cataclysmic events are done economically. In 1993 on the advice of soap innovator Phil Redmond, *Emmerdale* was given a make-over by the simple expedient of crashing a plane on the village. This wiped out many redundant characters. The plane crash took over three weeks to film at a cost of a million pounds, but such profligacy is rare. Whereas the episodic dramas dealt with in earlier chapters are generally shot on film and increasingly on HD. Soaps are always made on videotape with multi-camera set ups used to facilitate the recording of a lot of material per day. Soaps are enormously popular, economic and they consistently provide top ratings for schedulers. Pound for pound they are the most effective kind of TV drama. It is perhaps worth noting that the cost of a star actor's fees, if he or she has to be brought back after a near-death experience, is an area where soaps can be expensive.

EARLY DAYS

Soap opera began on American radio in the late 1920s. It soon became clear how popular it was and what a fine medium for selling well – soap. In 1935 Procter and Gamble (the giant American detergent manufacturer) invested two million dollars in soap opera. By 1939 the company had no less than twenty-one serials under its sponsorship, worth eight and three quarter million dollars, which today, using the consumer price index, is a staggering $124,462,855.06 (*see* www.eh.net/hmit).

In Great Britain, where there was no commercial radio, the soaps had a slower start. There was a wartime series *Front Line Family*, this was morale-boosting drama of everyday people. After the war this morphed into *The Robinsons* and in 1948 *Mrs Dale's Diary* began a 21-year run. *Mrs Dale's Diary*, renamed *The Dales* in the 1960s, was broadcast on the Home Service (the equivalent to BBC Radio 4). It ran for 5,531 episodes and ended on 25 April 1969. Hugely popular, it was identified by a harp glissando and Mrs Dale's: 'I'm worried about Jim [her husband]' became a much-loved catch phrase and a useful shorthand for comedians and parodists. As with *Hill Street Blues*, the musical sting and the catch phase were very important in the instant identification of the series.

The next radio soap was *The Archers*, which grew way beyond its original brief – to feed farmers nuggets of information from the 'Min. of Ag. and Fish'. It remains very popular today, though it now has considerably racier storylines. On the 12 of March 2004 it was the last long-running soap to have a gay kiss; it had taken 53 years. This storyline would have hardly raised a ripple in other soaps but in *The Archers* it made the National News. In November 2006, the time of writing this book, the Nation is still reeling from the near-infidelity of Ruth Archer with herdsman Sam on the 15,000th edition of the programme.

The BBC was always rather fastidious about soap opera and the radio soaps were introduced originally despite the opposition of the Drama Department.

> [Serials] are deliberately constructed to hit the very centre of the domestic hearth by playing variations upon the theme of all kinds of domestic trivia ...
>
> Val Gielgud, Director of Drama, BBC Radio, 1948

Val Gielgud, brother of Sir John, feared that their popularity would influence the quality of drama on BBC radio, corrupt the acting standards of the BBC repertory company and lay the Drama Department open to adverse criticism.

Despite its popularity, *Mrs Dale's Diary* was 'tolerated from a great height' and the BBC's fastidiousness continued into the age of TV. It was left to ITV to broadcast the first British TV soap *Coronation Street* in 1960. This began as a pilot written by Tony Warren called Florizel Street, a realistic slice of Northern working-class life. One of the working titles was *Where No Bird Sings*. Made by the Manchester-based Granada Television, it was initially not popular and many of the ITV regions refused to take it.

> The programme is doomed from the outset.
>
> Ken Irwin, *Daily Mirror*

But the show gradually took hold with ordinary viewers and sixteen episodes were made. They aired on 25 August 1960 and by October 1961, *Coronation Street* was the top-rating show in the country. This controversial slice of working-class life in a Manchester Street, which Warren had based on his experiences staying with his grandmother in Salford, became a national institution. It is still hugely popular and affectionately known as *Corry*.

Soap dominates early evening TV drama and consistently and reliably delivers excellent viewing figures. The health of soaps is discussed, particularly by TV execs and pundits, with a 'state of the nation' tone. Critics, however, tend to disguise admiration or even addiction to the genre behind a veil of pungent humour. Nancy Banks-Smith and Jim Shelley write both wittily and well about soap. Here is Nancy Banks-Smith on the death of the character Fred Elliott, who had first joined *Coronation Street* on 29 August 1994.

> In *Coronation Street* (ITV1) Fred Elliott dropped dead on his wedding day. I have seen several determined attempts to avoid matrimony, including legging it down the road in leg irons, but this was a soap first.
>
> Torn between two women, Fred (John Savident) was understandably in pieces. Though, frankly, you'd have thought there was enough of him to go round. Pale as a peeled egg, he fled the church before the bride arrived, to say goodbye to Audrey, the real love of his life. Saying, 'I'll not be seeing much of yer in the future,' he suited the word to the action and collapsed with a splintering crash on her escritoire. This sort of thing happens a lot to Audrey who, like Julius Caesar, prefers men about her that are fat. Her former husband, a portly grocer called Alf, also died suddenly on New Year's Eve, putting a bit of a damper on the celebrations.
>
> Nancy Banks-Smith, Tuesday 10 October 2006, *The Guardian*

In Great Britain, soaps have a place in the Nation's heart to the extent that no politician would dare to suggest he or she didn't like them. When news of the end of *The Dales* was announced, Liberal party MP Peter Bessell attempted to introduce a reprieve for the series in Parliament.

In 1998, Deirdre Rachid (Anne Kirkbride) in *Corry* was sentenced to eighteen months for credit card fraud. *The Sun* newspaper mounted a campaign with free stickers and T-shirts against this miscarriage of justice (Deirdre had been duped by a dodgy boyfriend). They claimed they had the backing of the Prime Minister. Tony Blair did indeed mention her case in the House of Commons – it wasn't clear if he was joking. One Labour MP went further. The Labour MP for Houghton and Washington East, Fraser Kemp, joined in the mania with a pledge to raise the 'clear miscarriage of justice' with Home Secretary Jack Straw. Mr Straw is quoted as saying it was a matter for the court.

In the 2001 election, Tony Blair was interviewed by real people about real problems on the set of the Channel Four soap *Brookside*. Since the audience was doubtless carefully screened by spin doctors, it makes your head ache trying to untangle the levels of reality involved with this situation. We have indeed come a long way from Val Gielgud's patrician dismissal. For the writer, the firm hold these characters have on the public imagination, and the great affection that even the villains are held in, must be taken seriously. The challenge, of course, is to inject your own voice without upsetting this magic.

While soaps may be taken seriously, and indeed must be by those who write them, they are not serious. They are essentially escapist and their roots lie in melodrama, where the peaks of dramatic action were highlighted by frantic scoring. Frantic scoring remains a feature of soaps to this day.

> No plot that you can't follow while getting the tea is any good.
>
> Mal Young

The Spine

A typical soap episode will have a main plot and several sub-plots. The main plot is often referred to as the spine, the backbone of that episode. The sub-plots fit in around it.

The Cliff

The cliff of an episode is generally marked out by storyliners. It is generally quite rigid. In *EastEnders* there was a phase of holding too long on the cliff. For example, a character discovers X is having an affair and she smashes up the windows of his car. The true cliff should be her discovery, as smashing up the windows takes impact out of it.

Let's examine this in relation to an episode of the New Zealand soap *Home and Away*. Here is a scene-by-scene breakdown of episode 4,066! See if you can spot the cliff in this episode.

6.00 pm Channel Five: Home and Away
Episode 4,066: Dr Jenkins Diagnoses Irene
1. *I'll knock his block off ...*
In the diner, we learn that Alf Ramsay is accused of fraud – diverting funds from surf club accounts. Morag urges caution.

2. *Oh God she left her mobile.*
Irene has not come back. Hayley, her pregnant daughter, worries.

3. *It's a plot ...*
In the diner, Alf says the accusation of fraud is a plot to discredit Alf's candidacy for post of Mayor of Summer Bay by Josh West (his opponent in the election). Others try to calm him.

4. *It's going to be dark soon.*
Sitting-room: characters worry about Irene. They decide to split up and search. Martha probes and Constable Corey opens up to her about his father committing suicide in prison. She makes sympathetic noises. We know that this a future love story subplot starting up. (In fact the sweet-faced trainee constable will turn out to be a poisoner.)

5. *There's her car ...*
EXT NIGHT (day for night): driving and looking Hyde and Hayley find Irene's car but no Irene. We see Irene in the bushes talking to someone.

6. *Don't lose it ...*
In the diner Alf is to do a radio interview the kids have fixed for him. He is warned not to lose his cool.

7. *I'm not going to hospital ...*
Irene wanders in, dishevelled with mysterious cuts. Despite her protests, she is taken to hospital.

Commercial Break

8. *Josh West set me up.*
In the diner, Alf is briefed on the radio interview. He must keep a cool head. But he blows it and libels Josh. The interviewer gets this all on tape.

9. *Let's get a photo of this ...*
In the bar, Josh West is campaigning. He is a smarmy bastard with a dodgy goatee attended by a photographer. He is schmoozing the local bowls club when the interviewer gets him on his mobile and plays Alf's accusations to him.

10. *I can guess where he's gone ...*
In the diner, Morag is berating Alf for the interview, when they hear Josh on the radio rebutting the charges and patronizing Alf. Alf storms out.

11. *No hard feelings ...*
Alf storms into bar. A confrontation and he hits Josh, who falls with a cut lip. The photographer snaps it.

12. *They all think I'm mad don't they ...*
In the hospital, Irene being patched up. She is clearly losing it. She doesn't seem to see Hayley and seems to be talking to an imaginary friend, Ken (a dead character). Doctors discuss her mental state.

13. *'Alf Pulls No Punches In Race For Mayor'.*
Next day. In the diner, they stare at this disastrous headline, and the photo of Alf punching out Josh.

14. *We must put her on drugs ...*
In the hospital, Dr Graham (a psychiatrist) uses the word 'psychosis'. We must put her on drugs till we find out what's going on.

15. *Get me out of here ...*
Irene says get me out of here, this trick cyclist is mad! Hayley: I don't know what's going on.

16. *Summer Bay is going to suffer.*
Josh West is elected overwhelmingly. Alf shakes his hand but aside says: Summer Bay is going to suffer.

17. *Project 56 is in the bag.*
Mayor's office night: sinister phone call. Josh West gloats, we don't know who he is talking to. He says 'Project 56 is in the bag'. A trailer says that we will know what Project 56 is before the end of the week.

This is a daily soap for kids and is a simple but very clear example of soap plotting. There are two plots running, nearly concurrently, and they are told in seventeen scenes. Ten scenes are devoted to Alf blowing the election (plot A) and seven scenes are devoted to Irene disappearing, being found and treated (plot B). There is also a strong signal of a third subplot (plot C) starting featuring Martha and Trainee Constable Corey. She persuades him to confide in her and she puts her arm around him. We know they will have a romance.

In half an hour we have two plots, either one of which could easily stretch to a 90-minute feature film. In different circumstances, we could imagine both the election-plot and the disturbed-mother-disappearing plot being extended over 90 minutes and in the case of Daft Dad Alf being a comedy or Mad Mum Irene being a tragedy. The soap doesn't do this. It's time-frame speeds through the incidents, using a kind of shorthand, for example, in scene 5, Hyde and Hayley are searching along the shore for Irene. In a feature film this might be an extended sequence with lots of tension – sinister shapes in the trees, the worried searchers, Irene muttering and crashing bloodily through branches. Instead it is reduced to three shots and lasts under two minutes. The plot is told as economically as possible because our real interest is what the characters are feeling and they are going to tell us about that. Subtext is seldom deeply buried in soaps, it nearly always bubbles to the surface at the slightest provocation. The challenge for the writer is to keep a clear grasp of where he has to get to for the next scene and place the action so that part one ends on a dramatic moment to hook the viewer back after the commercial break. In this, case scene 7, where the dishevelled and bloody Irene is made to go to hospital by her daughter.

Because this is a kids' show, many scenes are from the story point of view of the kids. The kids set up Alf's radio interview, they look anxiously at each other when he blows his top. It's the adults who need looking after. For the audience, the characters are familiar and we know what to expect of them. Daft Dad and Mad Mum are almost like family members and perhaps express in a safe way real fears – 'Dad will make a fool of himself and embarrass us, that's what he always does' and Mum, 'Well Mum, she's just bonkers!'. The soap completes the family circle of domestic viewing, however dramatic the events. they are generally brought back to simple basic human emotions. Even though the characters are in New Zealand. many thousands of miles away, a UK audience can see themselves in them. The cliff, by the way, is in beat 17 – 'Project 56 is in the bag'.

An Exercise

* Make your own scene breakdown of an early evening soap.
* How many plots can you detect?
* How many trailers for future plots?
* How many locations are used?
* Could you find a way to write any of these scenes more economically?

LATER THAT EVENING ...

The fundamental themes of soaps are explored as the evening goes on. The mood gets darker and the storylines mix in more violence and sex, yet there is always a strong familial undercurrent. At 6.30 pm in the teen soap *Hollyoaks*, girls talk about boys, dads worry about daughters, daughters again worry about dads. At 7.00 pm in *Emmerdale*, a girlfriend, thought mistakenly to be heartless, disrupts one family. Another family fights another over shares. A storyline that will culminate in über-bitch Sadie getting her comeuppance when she is tricked into eating her beloved horse Cossack with green pepper sauce. At 7.30 pm in *Coronation Street*, there are tensions between the parents of a single mother and her new boyfriend. A father and son tussle with the problem of whether to put grandpa, who is showing signs of dementia, into a home. In all these shows, despite very different locations, we are seldom far from the seven deadly sins dramatized in the domestic arena – family problems and the effects of unwise love.

There is a little playlet at the front of *Coronation Street*. The sponsors are Cadburys chocolates and the scene is of a family of real viewers sitting down to eat chocolate and watch TV. After the commercial break, more family members join them and by the end the sofa is full of chocolate-eating viewers. The scenario changes daily with a different set of real viewers from different parts of the country. TV soap puts us all on the sofa in the same family of chocolate-eating fans. Indeed the experience of watching a soap with a group of fans is a much more enjoyable experience than watching it on your own. As with football matches in pubs, as society fragments we like to use TV to be a catalyst to *ad hoc* communality.

In *EastEnders* at 7.30 pm 28 March 2006, we get a much more dramatic confrontation. Here, with the iconic Mitchell brothers, there is both the threat and the memory of violence.

> Because as we know, there are known knowns; there are things we know we know. We also know there are known unknowns; that is to say we know there are some things we do not know. But there are also unknown unknowns – the ones we don't know we don't know.
>
> Donald H. Rumsfeld, Department of Defense news briefing, 12 February 2002

1. *This is not a golf club ...*
The Mitchell brothers, Phil and Grant, arrive at an opulent house in Essex. Grant protests that this is not a golf club. Phil reveals it's his arch enemy, Johnny Allen's house. Phil says he is going to make J.A. confess. Grant tries to dissuade him. Phil gets back in the Range Rover but, instead of leaving, reverses it through the gates.

2. *I heard a noise ...*
In the house, Ruby, Johnny's daughter, who is making scones in the kitchen, hears a noise. Johnny says it is nothing. He goes into his office and swigs vodka secretly. Grant, pissed off with Phil, leaves him. Johnny sees Phil breaking in on CCTV.

3. *Stay in the office.*
Johnny shuts Ruby in the office and goes to sort out Phil. Ruby finds his secret stash of vodka. Johnny and Phil fight and Danny comes and helps. They are about to finish Phil off when Grant reappears and saves his brother. He effortlessly beats up Danny. Danny runs off. Johnny runs back into the office.

4. *You lied to me ...*
Ruby confronts her father with his secret drinking and smashes the bottles. Ruby wants nothing more to do with her Dad. She leaves him to Phil.

5. *Tea and sympathy ...*
Grant and Ruby have tea and scones, while in the office Phil tries to get a confession. He shows Johnny a video of Dennis battering Johnny and throwing him a mobile phone. Johnny knows that Phil encouraged Dennis to attack him and, says Phil, should be the one to feel guilty. In the kitchen, Ruby tells Grant what Phil did to Juley. Grant seems shocked.

6. *I'll ring Sharon ...*
Johnny admits to ordering Dennis' death. He says he will ring Sharon if it will make Phil feel better. His sneering pisses off Phil, who menaces him with a broken bottle.

And on this menacing action, the familiar drum beats end the episode.

The events in the episode are by any standards dramatic. The themes, a confrontation between violent men, a daughter discovering her father lied to her, two brothers falling out over how to handle their dangerous machismo, are worthy of Greek tragedy.

CONSISTENTLY INCONSISTENT

> [The character should be] consistent. If the model for the representation is somebody inconsistent, and such a character is intended, even so it should be consistently inconsistent.
>
> Aristotle, *The Poetics*

For the audience, the characters' actions are informed by back stories (*see* Chapter 7) that stretch back, in the case of the Mitchell brothers, more than ten years. Soap characters often swing backwards and forwards in the moral spectrum according to the demands of the story but they do this with the complicity of the audience. The fans know them so well – Oh, he's going to do that; Ah, but we know he'll do that. This ownership of the characters and the dramatic irony on display, because we know more about them than they know themselves, means the events are treated differently from the way they would be in say a Martin Scorsese film. Although violence is at the root of the behaviour of the male characters, as in *Goodfellas*, we don't see very much of it. This is partly because the show is broadcast quite early in the evening, when graphic violence, even if it could be afforded in the tight budget, would not be allowed by the broadcaster, and to make a character irredeemable would be impractical if you wanted to bring them back. But there is, I think, a deeper reason: the soap writer knows that his audience is really mainly interested in watching familiar characters ring changes on the character traits that they know so well (Rumsfeld's known knowns). Phil will explode, that's what he does, the question is when. Despite his new-found control, Grant will violently come through for his Bruv. When he's done this he, rather surreally, goes off with Ruby to drink tea in the kitchen leaving Phil alone with Johnny, possibly to beat him to a pulp. We are in the area of melodrama perpetually see-sawing between highs and lows – the writer is jerking our chain.

As in *Home and Away*, because the audience know the characters so well an awful lot of plot can be jammed into 30 minutes. The psychology and motivation of the characters is not explored in depth, it doesn't need to be. Subtext is replaced by the shared memory and people say what they mean, even when they are lying. The nature of soap is that the audience knows more than the characters.

When Ruby confronts her father in the office, he denies that the vodka she has found is his. 'The vodka is not mine, its Danny's' says Johnny. So Ruby smashes the bottles one at a time. As she prepares to smash the last bottle, Johnny cracks and admits he is an alcoholic. He says he will get help but Ruby, who we have seen in earlier episodes desperately trying to help him get a new life, cannot forgive him. She abandons him to the tender mercies of Phil. You could not really get away with this in any other genre; people would ask questions.

Long-running soap characters carry their back-story around with them in the same way that the actors, who play these characters, carry their roles. There is no escape, even in death. Both Phil and Grant have 'died' and left the series but, as with Sherlock Holmes, public pressure brought them back. Their every action is preceded by their histories. Here there is Phil's own struggle with alcohol, Grant's new found-ability to control his temper and the emotional scars of both Johnny's relationship with his daughter and her unhappy love affair with Juley, who Phil paid to seduce her. In soaps, the hard men's weakness is always their kids – that's how you get to them, that's where they show their vulnerable side.

FAMILY VALUES

The excitement of the events is curiously muted because the focus is much more on the emotional bonds between the characters. Father and daughter, brother and brother. Even Phil and Johnnie have their alcoholism in common. In the confrontation in the office, what really seems to get to Phil is that in the end Johnny is saying that Phil is no better than him. When driving to Johnny's house, when Grant urges his brother to get therapy and Phil mocks him, we are as disappointed as Phil. It is with relief when we see later on that Grant can still do the business when it's necessary.

The importance of defining characters through family is a reflection of a changing society. The absence of real communities leading to the creation of fictional communities. A group of people sitting watching a soap are enjoying a shared experience and both plot lines and past history contribute to this warm feeling. Even if the *EastEnders* or *Coronation Street* community is wish-fulfilment, it creates at least for half an hour a community of the sofa.

WHERE IS EASTENDERS?

Coronation Street does not exist anymore. *Corry* has dealt with this by pretending that there are still terraced streets like this. *EastEnders* seems to have just ignored the fact that the East End of London has changed. The East End is nothing like *EastEnders*. It's both gentrified while also being both deprived and more ethnically diverse than its fictional counterpart. There was in fact more diversity when the series began. That the posh people (or middle class) people are always the villains may be an unconscious reflection of how gentrification destroys communities as effectively as slum clearance in the 1950s and 60s destroyed the East End of the Blitz. Soaps' values are essentially conservative with a small 'c'. Their fans do not like change. The resistance to change is reflected even in the signature tune; when an attempt was made 10 years ago to make a 'jazzier' version (a bit like *Neighbours*), it had to be changed back because everybody hated it.

We talked earlier about iconic soap moments being landmarks in both the fans' and the characters' lives. Some examples of these are:

- Den serving Angie divorce papers on Christmas Day;
- 'Sharongate', where Sharon confesses on tape that she has been sleeping with Phil while married to Grant;
- 'You're not my mother, yes I am', Kat tells her sister Zoe that she is, in fact, her mother and was raped by her uncle.

The story beats in a single drama or in a single episode are mirrored by these big beats in a long-running show. We saw this when we looked at the beats in the love affair between Nate and Brenda in *Six Feet Under* over several episodes. As well as individual character arcs, there is the grand arc described by the whole show over many episodes, punctuated by these big beats. The orchestration of these is the true genius of storylining.

Despite this unreality, soaps do have a social responsibility. *EastEnders* introduced a character with HIV and therefore taught the Nation, that you don't have to be a gay drug-user to catch the disease. The ability to tackle 'issues' is at least for *EastEnders* very much part of the way it justifies itself.

Soaps are often said to be stories for women and, indeed, that's how they started off, but their radio heyday during the great depression set a template for a kind of drama that went for the emotional jugular, while at the same time massaged the dominant morality. Characters now are less unambiguously bad and good, but they still tend to get punished for their bad deeds in the end – though not all like Sadie in *Emmerdale* have to eat their pet horse!

WRITERS

What are soaps looking for when finding writers? The best soap writers write good characters with distinct voices. Ensemble soap drama, though often plot heavy, is at its best when character led. The successful writers on a soap (those allowed to cherry pick plots and write two or more episodes a month) have a very clear idea of the characters within the soap and what the audience expects from an episode. They are good at getting from A to B without it seeming contrived. You can tell their episodes when you watch as they have a deeper insight into the characters, and the pace of the scripts is noticeably quicker. The dialogue, as we said in the dialogue chapter, (*see* pages 48–58) fits the characters perfectly, so you recognize them and they act how you want them to.

An Exercise

You can find summaries of all *EastEnders* episodes on the BBC website (bbc.co.uk/eastenders). If you look at the summary of the episode on Tuesday 28 March 2006, you can try imagining this re-written by Quentin Tarantino for Martin Scorsese. See how the emotional point of view shifts when approached as a gangster movie and ask yourself, how is this different? And what does it tell you about our relationship with soap characters. What have you lost?

See if you can define the key beats and the scenes that in the soap get more weight. This will give you a clear idea of the kind of demands this sort of storytelling will make of you as a writer.

9 DEFINING AND SELLING YOUR STORY

If you are any kind of writer, people will regularly come up to you with their 'great idea for a movie, TV series, novel' and so on. Most people have stories to tell and everybody has one story – their own. What marks out the writer is the ability to work at that story, to use it, refine it, re-invent it and imagine it. There is no great trick to writing other than the ability, the discipline to sit down and do it. Of course there is the question of whether you have any talent for the trade, but that only time will tell. If you wish to turn your 'great idea for a TV series' into anything marketable, you are letting yourself in for a lot of work. It is best to shut up about your story till you have done that work.

In the preceding chapters, we have talked about the various formats for TV drama and I have analysed how some of the finest TV writers have dealt with aspects of plot, dialogue, character and time. What all these writers have in common is the ability to work and re-work, either alone or with their co-writers, their ideas. The process of defining and selling your story is the same for a single drama (TV movie) or a TV series. The difference is that with a series, there is much more work involved. To pitch a series you must not only have written the first episode (pilot) but have thought through and mapped out at least five plot-lines for subsequent episodes. These will show how the series and the characters develop. They will give the people you are pitching to an idea of the show's long-term potential.

LOG LINES

A log line encapsulates your story in a couple of sentences. I generally say no more than twenty-eight words. As well as being very useful as an answer to the question, 'What is this story about?', the exercise of trying to write a log line, which can and should continue as you write your script, is an excellent way to explore your story. It is impossible to pitch an idea, if you are not thoroughly acquainted with it. There is no better way to get to know your own story than to try to reduce it to those twenty-eight bare bones and still make it sexy. A log line, by its very compression, imposes a valuable discipline on the imagination. In this way it is like a haiku and, like a haiku, it should leave you wanting more.

> Late autumn
> A single chair waiting
> For someone yet to come
>
> Arima Akito

You will need your log line to pitch but the exercise of returning to it and refining it as you write your script, will help you to focus on what your script is really about.

How to Write a Log Line

Title. The title is outside your twenty-eight word ration, so make sure it is a good one. Does it evoke your story? Does it excite? Does it leave you curious and wanting more information? *Hill Street Blues. Six Feet Under. The Wire.*

Theme. What is the theme of your story? It is often the case that successful TV shows combine two themes, e.g. the family man who is also a gangster in The Sopranos.

Set The Scene. The precinct, a street in Manchester or the casualty ward of a big hospital.

Introduce the Characters. Give your characters good names. A name that resonates will work for you; a name that is merely a name will not pay its way. Making each word in the log line count and, if possible, count twice, prevents you being casual about naming your characters.

Colour, Taste and Smell. When you have to create the atmosphere of your story in just a few words, nothing is so good at doing this as adjectives that evoke colour, taste and smell.

Log-Line Exercise
- Try to write a log line for the series *Six Feet Under*. Maybe you can use the smell of embalming fluid or the theme of lives changed by sudden death. What do the names of the characters tell you, if anything?
- Write a log line for your favourite TV show.
- Write a log line for your show.

YOUR STORY

Is my story any good? How can I make it popular? Is it worth telling? Is it true or false? Does it have the makings of a hit? These frequently asked questions can only ever be turned back on you. It is true that nobody knows anything and that success is unpredictable, but unless you believe in what you are doing, then you will be unlikely to be able to sell it. Let us assume that you wish to turn your 'great idea for a script' into a spec script, the pilot for a potential series. Here are some of the questions that it should answer or be answered by

97

the other materials (character biographies, synopses of future episodes) you present with it. Go back to the headings of the previous chapters and use them to critique your ideas.

The Audience Bond

This is a scripturgical phrase, I think originated by Robert McKee, that you will hear. What it means is the way a writer ties an audience to a character. How can a character like Othello be attractive? How can we be repelled yet fascinated by Hannibal Lecter?

My belief is that a writer must love his characters. However vile they are, unless they are written with love, they will not bond with the audience. There is a very good example of this in *The Sopranos'* episode *College*, which I discussed in Chapter 7, written by James Manos Jr and David Chase. In this episode, Tony is taking his daughter Meadow to look over Colby College when he spots stool-pigeon Fabian Petrulio who is now living, under witness protection, as Frederick Peters with a wife and young daughter. Tony realizes that he has to kill Petrulio and that is something he must not delegate – because of the mafia code, he must do the murder himself. Throughout the superbly written episode, the two moral imperatives, looking after his daughter and worrying about her college place, see-saws with Tony's eventually successful attempts to kill Peters. Our empathy with Tony remains strong throughout. We can all identify with his fears for his daughter but few of us have first-hand experience of whacking a mafia stoolie. Neither moral imperative is flinched, instead they are both pushed to the limit. Tony's killing is as brutal and cold blooded as his nervousness about his daughter's future and his desire to protect her is genuine. The writers skilfully keep both balls in the air, so in the end we are placed firmly at the heart of Tony's moral schizophrenia. Our bond with him stays intact.

In general your characters will bond with your audience in direct proportion to your commitment to them. If they are mere ciphers for either your moral or your theme, the audience will not warm to them and certainly not take them to their hearts.

Plot

What's the plot? Does it engage? Is it exciting, funny? Does the set up, your first act, put you clearly in the world of the story and make you want to know more? Think of the trolley crashing through the emergency room doors in *ER*. Or the satellite that takes a crucial phone call halfway across the world in *24*. Does your pilot satisfactorily conclude its plot but still leave doors open for future episodes? Have you placed at least one subplot, preferably two? Have you laid the seeds of romance or even treachery?

Character

Can you see and hear the characters? Are some characters introduced briefly who have the potential for development in later episodes? Think of that first entrance of Robbie Coltrane in *Cracker* or Fiona in *Shameless*. Is there a convincing character arc to your main character? Bear in mind that this may not become apparent till future episodes, but do we see a man or a woman launched on either a physical or a mental journey. Do you yourself like them enough to stay with them over many episodes, because if you don't nobody else will.

Dialogue
What is the vernacular of your story? What language do your characters speak? What is their mother tongue? Is it a clearly defined region of your own country like *Boys from the Blackstuff* or *Heimat*, or is it cop-speak or doc-speak. Again, can you hear your characters? If you are unfamiliar with their way of speaking, what steps have you taken to immerse yourself in their world? Do your characters speak among themselves in a private language that reinforces their world? Have you made sure that in presenting this accurately you haven't excluded your audience?

Structure and Dynamics
Are you able to pre-figure the structure of the continuing series in your first episode – your pilot? When the municipal bus hits Nathaniel Fisher's hearse in episode one of *Six Feet Under*, causing the accidental death of the proprietor and owner of Fisher and Sons Funeral Homes, it brings the scattered family together, literally, round the coffin. It is the inciting incident for this episode but it also provides the template for all the subsequent episodes. In each of these, we begin with a death. We go on through the mechanics and the ritual of the funeral to explore both the lives of the relatives of the corpse but also the lives of our permanent characters. In other words the pilot creates the format. Does your pilot do this or do subsequent episodes not follow a pattern? If the answer is 'No', then you should ask yourself what is the theme or character that gives continuity to future episodes.

> Watson insists that I am the dramatist in real life. Some touch of the artist wells up within me, and calls insistently for a well-staged performance. Surely our profession would be a drab and sordid one if we did not sometimes set the scene so as to glorify our results.
>
> Sherlock Holmes in *The Valley of Fear* by Conan Doyle

Detective stories have always been a staple of all kinds of drama. In TV terms they have an in-built format. A crime is committed and a detective is asked to investigate, the episode will therefore follow the course of that investigation. Subsequent episodes will also follow a similar blueprint.

In a crime series, murder might kickstart the format but in a medical drama like *House*, a sick patient's mysterious disease can do the same. The disease becomes the crime, Dr House the brilliantly intuitive detective. The mechanics of his diagnosis and cure is the weekly format. A detective story in white coats.

The questions you must ask yourself of your pilot are:

- What is the inciting incident?
- Does it kickstart events and create the structure?
- Is that structure dynamic?
- Will it sustain?
- How does the structure impact on the theme of your series?

There is a bloody murder that starts the episode. If it is particularly upsetting, does it affect the supposedly detached cops, emotionally? Does it, for example, involve one of them as a suspect? You have to ask these questions of yourself because, as I said at the beginning of the chapter, they will be thrown back at you. Get a friend to play Devil's Advocate and role-play an executive asking awkward questions. You can never predict these with certainty but if you have successfully answered searching questions, it will give you much greater confidence when facing the real thing.

Time

BOCHCO: *Hill Street Blues* might have been the first television show that had a memory. One episode after another was part of a cumulative experience shared by the audience. Something that happened in the 100th episode had 99 hours of history behind it. We were able to communicate more information by implication in an hour episode than anyone had done before, because our storylines as well as the characters had grown and evolved over years. Your knowledge and memory of any given episode was informed by your experience watching previous shows.

What is the time frame of your pilot? Do you have to include back-story information? How is this told? Voice-over? Flashback? Do you maintain tension in the scenes where you give the audience this vital information? Are the scenes you have written memorable? If you wish to originate a long-running series, your job is partly to create fictional memories for your audience. Laying the foundations of events that you may not even guess at now. Do the incidents of the pilot strike you as suitable foundations? If we think of the death of Nathaniel Fisher, we see that this inciting incident changes everybody's life. This highly dramatic moment will both be a strong memory for the fictional characters and a rich seam for the writers of future episodes to draw on. The question you must ask yourself is, are you providing your audience with something as strong?

Pitching

Lieber Freund, entschuldige meinen langen Brief,
für einen kurzen hatte ich keine Zeit.

Charlotte von Stein an Johann Wolfgang von Goethe

This translates as, 'Sorry for sending such a long letter, I didn't have the time to write a short one'. The work required to create your brief and exciting pitch from whatever material you have, is central to the art of pitching. Pitching is selling. Whatever the situation, you as writer will find yourself selling your story and therefore yourself to someone. You may be doing this as part of a team or you may be on your own. You may be in an office, a restaurant or a urinal, you are still pitching.

There is an acre of advice on this subject, some of the best in my view is on WGA website and in Julian Friedman's excellent book *How to Make Money Scriptwriting*. Elsewhere there is a lot of bad and confusing advice and I am reluctant to elaborate too much. Keeping it simple is in any case a very good motto when pitching.

Know Your Story

The more you know your subject, the more concise and entertaining your pitch can be. Even if what you present is two pages or only twenty-eight words (a log line), it should represent a great deal of work. The American advice is to leave nothing behind, this way there can be no second thoughts as your piece of paper goes through various grubby fingers, as it is handed from executive to executive. However in my experience in the UK, if interest is shown and you are asked to, it is advisable to follow it up as soon as possible with a couple of pages outlining the idea. This is easy to do because you will have already done the background work. It is always best to do this as soon a possible. Strike while the iron is hot because TV executives can blow with the wind (the changing brief from on high) and quite often seem to have the attention span of gnats. Solid work on your story is always money well spent, if not necessarily money in the bank.

Know Your Audience

Both in the sense of who you are pitching to and who your story is for. Research the producer and the company you are pitching to. The more you know about them, the more you will be able to initiate a dialogue. By asking questions of them you can get them to ask questions of you. Once they do ask a question, then they have opened a door.

Have Something Else Ready. Always have a second idea so that if they ask you if you have anything else, you can say, 'Yes I have'.

Never Apologize. Be neither humble nor boastful about your work. If you don't believe in yourself, it's hard, if not impossible, to get somebody to believe in you.

Keep It Simple. Do not over-elaborate. The work you have done should be like the six-sevenths of the iceberg. It should convey that behind your pointed and gleaming pitch, there is a solid foundation of real work.

Bait The Hook. The best pitches show 'the money' a window on the real world. Give them something concrete to hang on to. 'Some years ago I fell in love with a girl in a red dress.' 'Did you know that eighty percent of serial killers were terrified of bananas?' Bait the hook, invent if you have to, after all that is your job.

Checklist for Pitching
- Know your story.
- Know your audience.
- Have something else ready.
- Never appologize.
- Keep it simple.
- Bait the hook.

COPYRIGHT

Once you have written something you have established your copyright. You do not need to produce it at the interview, indeed it is advisable not to, but its existence will prevent your brilliant idea for a series being borrowed. The fact that you have an already written script, synopsis or episode outline will protect you.

Writers often worry unnecessarily about copyright; it is a vast and complex subject and constantly changing with technology – it would take many books to cover it. So what I will do is try to describe the concept of copyright and then tell you where to get more information. Once you have grasped the basic principle, you will, hopefully, be less afraid of people stealing your work.

There are two golden rules.

- Never sign anything you don't understand.
- Never sign anything, even if you think you understand it.

The implications of what may appear at first sight to be perfectly reasonable, need to be examined by a professional (*see* below).

What is Copyright?
Copyright, as the word suggests, is the right to protect your copy. Copy here is used in the newspaper sense – the words you have committed to paper. In other words, by the very virtue of having written your screenplay, you have copyrighted it. This, of course, also applies to a short story or a novel, or for that matter a piece of music or a painting. So if you wander around telling everybody your great idea for a movie, don't be surprised if someone else writes it. Keep quiet, lock yourself away, sit down and write it. You cannot copyright ideas or titles. In order to gain copyright protection, your screenplay must be original, but if you have reworked the thriller with the cop with the busted marriage and the drink habit, relax. The law in this sense defines originality as the skill and

hard graft you have put into your screenplay. If original meant 'innovative and of cultural merit' most films would get sued. In practice it is cheaper for a studio to buy your script than to steal it. The stealing comes later on and is all perfectly legal; that's why you need an agent or lawyer to protect you when you come to signing a contract. You will be amazed at how easy it is to get one of these, the moment anybody wants to pay money for your screenplay.

Paranoia

As I have said, the fact that you have written your screenplay protects you, and to a certain extent, your ideas are protected too. In the UK, the Right of Confidentiality says that if I (the writer) come to you (the producer) with an idea designed for our mutual benefit (a screenplay), then the person who is the recipient (the producer) cannot exploit it to the exclusion of the initiator (the writer). In practice, in the UK and Europe you and your work are well protected, but beware – you have to exploit the idea. If you write your screenplay and keep it in a drawer for some years and someone then makes a similar film, you won't have a leg to stand on.

Registering Your Work

The countries of the EC have harmonized their copyright laws (although there are differences of detail), so that broadly speaking they provide protection for the lifetime of the writer, his children and grandchildren (seventy years from the death of the author). In the USA, copyright is designed as protection for the life of the work; i.e. EC law protects the writer's family, and US law protects the work itself. The fashion for registering your work comes from the USA where, because copyright is based on the life of the work, it is important to register the 'birth' of the work. Although US law has recently been amended to conform more to the European model, it is coloured by its history and still carries the requirement of registration.

Registering your work merely proves that you wrote it at a certain time. It does not increase your copyright. In the very unlikely case of your screenplay being the subject of a court case, this could just be useful. Its main effect is to remove writer's paranoia and leave him or her free to concentrate on the main task of writing and selling the screenplay.

Some Things You Can Do

Make sure your work bears a copyright symbol © followed by your name and the year it was created. If you are really paranoid, send a copy by registered post to your bank, accountant or your lawyer with special instructions to hold the envelope unopened in safe-keeping. In that way you can produce evidence as to when your work was written, which would be of value in the unlikely event of somebody coming up with a substantially similar work (the earlier work would take precedence). For further advice, the WGGB (Writer's Guild of Great Britain) has an excellent website (www.writers.org.uk/guild/), which not only has essays on copyright to which again we are indebted but also has links to the WGA (Writer's Guild of America). If you want, the WGGB will register your script free of charge. USA copyright advice is available from the US Government website. The WGGB site also has details of minimum terms agreements with the BBC, PACT (independent producers) and ITV. If you are a member of BECTU, they still have a registration service.

If you use the *Final Draft* program, you can connect from the program to ProtectRite (www.protectrite.com) and they will charge you a fee (at the time of writing $18) to register your script on-line with them.

For more information see *The Writers and Artists Year Book*, where there are excellent essays on UK and US copyright law. For those who wish to dip their toes into this fantastically complex subject, there is another excellent book, *A User's Guide to Copyright* by Flint, Fitzpatrick and Thorne (Butterworths). This is a 600pp. work, the first two hundred pages of which are fairly easy for a non-lawyer to understand. But they won't make you a better writer.

If you are writing a script for an independent producer, you will be required to assign the whole of the copyright in the work to the producer, and if you are writing for the BBC you will be required to grant a licence for the full period of copyright. The difference between these two circumstances is more than might appear but, since the position is likely to be non-negotiable, may be regarded as of little concern to you. What should be of much greater concern is the difference between a script that forms part of a series created by someone else, and an original piece of work, whether a one-off or a pilot for a series.

The various minimum terms agreements generally only address the position of where the writer does not own the 'format'. The 'format' (a concept with which lawyers often find some difficulty) may be described as the expression of an original idea for a television programme consisting of such elements as its setting, characters and their relationships, its themes and how the general narrative might develop. You may have to grant extensive rights in the script, but you would expect only to grant a licence of much more limited rights in the format. If the television series was very successful you might want to write a novel, a stage play or a movie based on the format, although not replicating the television script, as such. In rare cases there can be significant value in licensing the 'changed format' rights, i.e. the right to make a new American or German version of the UK series (as opposed to selling the original series to those territories).

It is of course possible that you might write an episode of a series created by someone else, but nevertheless create in your script an entirely new character who the producers might wish to re-use. You need to make sure that provision is made to protect your interests in this circumstance, e.g. the BBC own the format in *Dr Who*, but Terry Nation owns the Daleks. With the series *Baxter*, which I mentioned earlier, as I wrote the scripts, they were my copyright but the format rights, because we developed it jointly, were shared fifty-fifty between Nigel and myself. Our agents then assigned the copyright in the format and the scripts of *Baxter* to the commissioner of the series, in this case Pearson TV.

The format might be looked on in relation to the various scripts, in the same way that a novel relates to the screenplay based on it from which a movie is made. Lawyers may struggle with the concept of format because there is no reference to it in the Copyright Act, but agents should not. Thus unless you are a lawyer, and not just any lawyer but a specialist in media law, you will need an agent.

Remember again the two golden rules:

- Never sign anything you don't understand.
- Never sign anything even if you think you understand it.

And get advice.

AGENTS

What is an agent? An agent represents you and negotiates the licensing of your work, your contracts. As a screenwriter you will need an agent and there are no short cuts to obtaining one. An agent will take a percentage of your fee to see that you get a good deal. In the UK this is between 10 and 15 per cent and is tax deductible. It will be money well spent.

As well as negotiating your fee, a good agent will advise and suggest ways your script may be improved or steered towards a more likely area of the marketplace. Obviously this is a delicate and potentially explosive task but it is not unusual for a writer to walk into his agent's office thinking he has written a romantic comedy and, without necessarily changing a word, come out realizing he has written a thriller!

An agent has both a creative and a financial incentive to send a screenplay to people who will exploit it. And to match your work with producers, studios and actors.

How to Get an Agent

There are, as I have said above, no short cuts. Obtain a list of agents. Most, together with descriptions of the kind of work they handle, are listed in *The Writer's and Artists Yearbook*. Or you could try typing 'literary agents' into your search engine. However, many of these will not handle screenplays but represent novelists and authors of travel, cookery or other works. You will need to find out whether the agency represents screenwriters. The Personal Managers Association (PMA) will send you a list (Info@thepma.com).

You must ring the agency first to see if they represent screenwriters and if they read unsolicited scripts. If they do, send a copy of your screenplay. Pick three agents and follow their instructions as to what they want you to send them, enclosing a stamped addressed envelope, if they request one. If rejected, send a fresh script to another agent, as there may be coffee stains and pencil marks on the returned script – a good sign, indicating that it has been read. If they give you any hope, asking to see your next work for example, follow it up. Keep a list or database that tells you what you have sent where. Always have three scripts out. Deal with the problem of three agents who want to represent you, should it arise.

PRODUCERS

Whether you succeed in getting an agent or not, you will require a producer. Indeed the search for a producer should be carried on while you are looking for an agent. You go about it in much the same way, that is by research, and targeting someone who is right for your screenplay. Up till the time of getting a producer you are your own producer. It is you who sends out the script and tries to interest people in the programme.

Options

A producer will frequently option a book. This means that he or she buys the right for a given period, say six months to two years, to exploit the book by having it adapted for TV. Options, unless they are for a best-seller, are comparatively inexpensive but for a book to be exploited, it needs to be turned into a script. The producer will try and get the money to commission a writer to adapt the book. Most adaptations, therefore, are commissioned work, but if you decide to adapt a novel on spec, it is essential that you secure the rights – an option on the novel – otherwise all your work will be in vain. The first thing any producer or production company wants to know is, who owns the rights.

ON ADAPTATION

> He hadn't read the novel, but it was clear that he had once been in a room with someone who had read it.
>
> Barry Hanson (producer) on a commissioning editor

The reason that so many dramas on TV are adapted novels is that a book is a known commodity. Two-thirds of all the movies ever made have been adaptations, and the same is true for television. The creative slog and, to a certain extent, the creative risk have already been taken, so for those working in development, adaptation makes perfect sense.

If the book has been a success then the film can hitch a ride on that success, making marketing a lot easier. While adapting a successful novel is never a sure fire recipe – the TV version of Zadie Smith's novel *White Teeth* springs to mind – the novel adaptation both historical/'classic' like *Pride and Prejudice* or contemporary like *The Line of Beauty* remains increasingly a staple of TV drama. The novel spreads the risk in a way that original work doesn't. As costs escalate and producers become more and more reluctant to gamble on original work, the number of adapted novels on TV increases.

Do adaptations have any place in a book about creative TV writing? The great French screenwriter, Jean Claude Carrière is famous for saying that the way to adapt a novel is to read it once and then put it under your chair and allow its scent to rise up as you type. This is better advice than cut and paste, for what you must have in your head as you work is a clear emotional response to the book. This is the only way 200,000 odd words can be converted into a 20,000-word screenplay and be a rewarding project for the screenwriter. It is also where the creative aspect of adapting comes into play. For, when re-telling a story in another medium, creative decisions and creative leaps have to be made at almost every stage of the process.

> I don't want to cram in sex, or ... er guns or car chases ... you know or characters growing or learning profound life lessons or coming to like each other, or overcoming obstacles to succeed in the end. The book isn't like that you know and life isn't like that ... I feel very strongly about this.
>
> *Adaptation* (screenplay Charlie Kaufman and Donald Kaufman, director Spike Jonze)

The quote above is spoken by the fictionalized 'Charlie Kaufman' (Nicholas Cage) in *Adaptation*, in reply to the executive (Tilda Swinton), who is asking him to adapt the novel *The Orchid Thief*, and represents the writer's principled position. In the film, of course, he is then given the job and ... well I won't spoil the film for you.

The first thing you have to establish is what the producer or television company think they have bought. That tender love story that brought a tear to your eye has been read by the producer as a slasher movie or acquired as a vehicle for a totally inappropriate actor, who is currently bankable. The book, whatever it is/was and however it has affected the adapter, has becomes a commodity. He or she must now turn it into the drama the producer wants.

My first adaptation was a Franz Kafka novel, *America*, for a fringe theatre in the 1970s. I bought two copies of the novel, ripped one up and literally cut and pasted the bits together with rudimentary stage directions and work-shopped the whole mess with the actors. It eventually worked reasonably well, mainly thanks to the actors but also, as I discovered when we started to perform the play, because almost nobody has read Kafka's *America*. I was able to write whole scenes that weren't in the novel and several people told me how true I'd been to the author's text. Though this is a good example of beginner's luck, it is not a good method for working.

When I adapted Minette Walter's *The Scold's Bridle* for the BBC, I had to reconstruct a complicated and difficult book and turn it into two 75-minute episodes. What informed everything I wrote was Minette's central image of the scold's bridle, a medieval device for imprisoning a woman's tongue. This was used in the book both as the historic instrument but also as a wider metaphor for silencing women. In the story it represented a legacy of abuse, handed down from one generation to another. Keeping this strong central theme in my head (what Carrière called 'the scent of the book') was more important than technical factors like shifting the climaxes of the first half of the book in order to have a dramatic end to episode one.

Sometime after the broadcast, I was trying to collect some thoughts about adaptation for a script workshop. Prompted by hearing the novelist P.D. James criticize one of her adapters in a radio interview, I wrote to Minette asking if she could judge the reaction of her fans. Did they see the television drama as a travesty of the novel? This was her reply:

> In terms of your suggestion that adaptations for the fans are bound to be a travesty, I am always fascinated by the letters I get from people who have seen the adaptation and then read the book. Invariably they say the book is better ... nevertheless this is not in my view a valid criticism of the adaptation ... . From an author's point of view – and of course I am speaking for myself – I watch adaptations of my work only as television. Does it make good television? Is it gripping? Is it good drama?

Two kinds of morality tend to be invoked when discussing the pros and cons of adaptations. Firstly, they occupy space that could be devoted to original work and second, that in some way adaptations damage or pollute the original works on which they were based. The first, while undoubtedly true, is a fact of life that we have to live with for the reasons that I have stated above. The second is answered in this way. Great works of art like *Crime and Punishment* or *Romeo and Juliet* are very robust. Shakespeare in particular can survive anything. There have been numerous dreadful productions of his plays since his death but he is still going strong. With regard to modern novels, as any publisher will tell you, a television or film adaptation sends their sales figures rocketing. There are very few people who won't read a book because they've seen it adapted on television. Even if only one new reader is gained, and that reader thinks the adaptation a shallow rendering of a profound masterpiece, the novelist is in all senses better off.

Some novels are improved through adaptation. Leaving aside all the pulp thrillers and *série noir* novels that have become excellent movies (such as *The Wages of Fear*), let's take an example nearer to a modern classic. Christopher Hampton's masterly adaptation of Malcolm Bradbury's *The History Man* gave it a shine none of Bradbury's later televised works received; a magic that Hampton, as adapter and translator, has worked on several other authors.

What does a novel provide for the adapter? The hard creative labour has been done and ideas, character and plot are all there to be plundered. Due to the greater length of a novel, and its ability to weave commentary and explore characters' minds, characters are often well-developed as parts for actors. Even before a word of the adaptation is written, it is possible to ask an actor's agent whether their client would like to play Zhivago. Nobody needs to have read the book.

What does a novel not provide for an adapter? Few novelists write convincing dramatic dialogue. F. Scott Fitzgerald and Hemingway wrote dialogue that sings on the printed page but becomes curiously lumpen when given to actors to speak, unlike Graham Greene whose ear for dramatic dialogue was not lost when he wrote novels.

Often novelists will omit what are key scenes for the adapter. Andrew Davies, who adapted *Dr Zhivago* for ITV mentions Pasternak's infuriating habit of not writing the key scenes and speaks eloquently of searching in vain for the crucial Lara/Komarovsky seduction. This is a crucial scene for a screen-writer but not for the novelist who can leap from A to C, even from A to F with a single bound. The novelist can go from one place in the action to another by describing, through the character's thoughts, the psychological effect that the physical or temporal journey has had on them. What interested Pasternak was not that Lara was seduced: 'Lara walked all the way home in a daze and only realized what had happened to her when she got home.' Pasternak wrote what was for him the important sentence. Lara unpicks the memory of what has happened to her and realizes that she is now a fallen woman. The reader fills in the gaps.

Davies says that Lara is both fascinated and revolted by Komarovsky and this drives her into a disastrous marriage just to escape from him, but there is no scene that shows this. The dramatic moment is missing and the adapter's job is to create one. In this instance Davies did this by having Lara take the lead in her own seduction when she opens the door. The French call this the *scène à faire* – the one you've got to write.

What is meant by the dramatic moment? In all dramatic scenes there is a significant moment. To quote Raymond Chandler, 'When in doubt have a man come through a door with a gun'. Of course it's not always a gun; sometimes it's a love letter opened, a door unlocked or a kiss surprised. These are the hooks on which actors hang their performances and audiences their expecta-tions. Not all novelists have these moments, and when they do, they are not always in the right place. The adapter's job is to move the scene and if the scene is not there to create it.

Often the way we eavesdrop on a character's thoughts is what gives reso-nance to a novel. It may appear that the adapter has a direct equivalent of this in the voice-over but the way we hear a character speaking in our heads when we read is very different from the way we hear a voice-over. This is because the main dialogue in a novel is between the characters' thoughts and the images the author creates in our minds. In a TV drama these images are supplied, so the voicing of thoughts becomes not active, as it is in the novel, but passive. To comment on images already seen is redundant and makes the story plod.

Of course it is possible to replace the first-person narrative of a novel with voice-over, but the very fact that this is the most obvious device should warn the writer not to use it straight away. Voice-over can be used creatively and I have discussed its use in Chapter 7, but even if it is the most obvious device, it is often too literal and indeed too literary.

The novel *The Scold's Bridle* is dominated by the diaries of the dead woman, Mathilda, sections of which are interspersed throughout the text creating a kind of chorus to the main action. To quote Minette Walters: 'In *The Scold's*

Bridle, I was determined to give my corpse a voice in order to be able to offer two truths at the end of the story – i.e. the 'judicial' truth: who murdered who and why; and the real truth: what made Mathilda a victim.'

As an adapter, I had a choice between a narrative heavily dominated by voice-over (the diaries), which would have perhaps made for a more subtle piece, and a narrative relentlessly driven by the murder plot. I took the decision to use only one section of the diaries, to 'top and tail' the piece. The film began and ended with a Mathilda voice-over and a single flashback to her horrific childhood. In order to cannibalize some of the resonance of the diaries, I filched many of the best lines from them and gave them to other characters – principally her daughter, played by Trudie Styler. In this way I turned the 'voice' of the novel from passive to active. A study of non-communication became a crime story dominated by the damage caused by sexual abuse.

Most adapters begin with a feeling of respect for the original work as they recognize another writer's toil and craft. Paradoxically that respect can leave an adapter troubled at the end when reflecting on the appropriateness of his/her creative choices. It must always be remembered that the adapter's primary responsibility is always to the drama.

Exercises
- Read the novel as a reader and remember your initial response.
- Make a breakdown of the novel, similar to a step outline, marking it with page numbers of the novel for easy reference.
- Write the story again for the TV medium. Referring to your breakdown rather than the original novel.
- Use the page numbers to cannibalize what you want or need.
- Respect the original novel but do not be inhibited by your respect. Remember you have to make it work in a different medium and so anything goes. If you must invent scenes and dialogue then invent them.

10 FIVE LESSONS FROM COMEDY

THE DEFINITION OF COMEDY

> Comedy is a representation of an action that is laughable and lacking in magnitude, complete [in embellished speech] with each of its parts [used] separately in the [various] elements [of the play]; [represented] by people acting and [not] by means of narration; accomplishing by means of pleasure and laughter the catharsis of emotions. It has laughter [so to speak] as its mother.
>
> (I explained what each of these things means when tragedy was defined.)
>
> Aristotle's *Poetics II* translated by Richard Janko

I went for a drink once with a producer I was working with. As we entered the bar, he waved to two dejected people who sat in silence with a crumpled pack of crisps between them staring into their beer. They emanated such an air of silent misery that I asked the producer who they were. 'Oh they're the comedy writers.' Comedy is a serious business.

It is perhaps the best joke of all that Aristotle's *Poetics II*, which dealt with comedy, has been lost. Scholars have, with varying degrees of success, attempted to reconstruct it. The quote above comes from Richard Janko's 1987 *Aristotle's Poetics*, in my view the only readable translation of this work. The absence of a clear guideline from the great Greek philosopher means that we will be spared a Robert McKee of comedy. Though there is plenty of advice out there, David Evans' *The Seven Laws of Comedy Writing* are, while not exactly laws, useful guidelines.

Even defining comedy is as elusive as bottling fog. For a start, what one person will find hilarious another will not laugh at at all. There is no worse experience than a good friend showing you a DVD, 'Watch this, this will kill you'; but for you the gags do not connect or you don't get the concept. The more your friend laughs the more stony-faced you become. Laughter and its absence can kill friendship and end a love affair. It's powerful stuff and comedy writers know when they have succeeded because the audiences laugh. Writers of drama and tragedy can debate up to a point whether an audience is moved or not; comedy writers have no place to hide.

The types of comedy on TV are to a large extent divided into those that are recorded before a live audience, like *Red Dwarf*, and those that are filmed or taped like other types of drama without an audience, like *The Thick of It*. It's interesting that the first show has a cast of comedians, who often find it easier to work with a live audience, and even in some cases impossible to 'act' without one, whereas the second has a cast of actors. The actors will begin with the characters and build the comedy from the way they play those characters. The live audience for the conventional sitcom, which is a taped show on a few sets before a studio audience, is a different beast from the comedy drama, which has perhaps a larger canvas, more sets or locations and more character development.

Laughter is an inclusive activity, you need at least one other person to create it. The audience is often crucial to the ability of some performers to perform. All actors feed off a live audience and comedy actors are no exception. The limitations of studio-based shows, few sets, multi-camera set ups and many more minutes a day, is more than made up for by the buzz the performers get off the audience. Many comedians turned actors find it virtually impossible to perform without the adrenalin-rich situation of the live audience.

In *Curb Your Enthusiasm*, although there is no live audience, the effect of immediacy is created by the adrenalin of improvised dialogue in which, within certain limits, anything can happen. For the most part, the cast who are stand-up comics, respond better to this than they would to performing scripted lines. You could say that the 'fourth wall', the audience, has to be replaced by something. This is either the adrenalin of improvisation or a scripted context that contains the characters in a context that the audience feels comfortable with.

The great success of *The Office* was enormously helped by the fact that audiences felt instantly in an environment they recognized. Anyone who had ever worked in an office felt at home in this world. It was set where the majority of the audience worked.

In the USA, they make a distinction between the ensemble show – *Jack Benny*, *The Muppets* – and the family show – *The Cosby Show*, *The Simpsons* or *Friends*. Often the ensemble show is a disguised sketch show. Kermit the Frog, the master of ceremonies, presides over an unruly bunch of characters who do their sketches one after the other. It is in the case of *The Muppets*, a show within a show. A venerable and of course, because you can have guest stars, infinitely variable format.

The UK series *Green Wing* is an interesting case. This very funny disguised sketch show, set in an anarchic hospital, gradually began to accrue more and more plot till the last episode of the last series became essentially comedy drama. In other words, the characters had moved from merely doing gags to having a personality of their own. Something similar happened with *The Muppets* with the leitmotif of the 'love affair' between Miss Piggy and Kermit. The unexpected humanity of puppets and cartoons, their capacity to move us, is often disconcerting. The Simpson family is a case in point.

FIVE LESSONS FROM COMEDY

Let's look back on our chapters and examine comedy under the headings of pilot, character, dialogue, structure and time. As I said at the beginning, I think comedy writers have a lot to teach us.

Pilot

The more you examine the genesis of successful UK comedy shows, the more you find that their births were never straightforward. *Only Fools and Horses*, arguably the most successful British sitcom ever, took some time to establish itself. It was finally helped by the three-day week, when a stalled Great Britain had nothing else to watch. Perhaps more fundamentally, writer John Sullivan's Del Boy reassured the audience that British talents for ducking and diving, with its echoes of a wartime spivs and the black market, would see the country through this new 'darkest hour'. Again, we find a character who seems to fit an actor like a glove, yet David Jason was far from the first choice to play the title role. However, he played it incomparably and fixed both himself and the character in the nation's heart.

Porridge written by Dick Clement and Ian La Frenais began life as a single play, *Prisoner and Escort* featuring an escaped convict Fletcher on the loose in Dartmoor. It was only when Fletcher was contained mainly in his cell in Slade Prison that Ronnie Barker's interpretation of Clement and La Frenais' character took wing. Somehow the more he was confined, the freer he was, indeed they all were.

The pilot of *The Office* was re-made and it was only the second pilot that clicked. The pilot, or at least first episode of the first series, of *Black Adder* by Richard Curtis and Rowan Atkinson was re-made and the lost pilot, which was never seen by an audience exists allegedly as a ropey VHS or can be downloaded by the dedicated through Bit Torrent. It is a frequent topic of Net obsessives, though perhaps not quite as big a topic as the 'lost' *Buffy* pilot! Aristotle must be chortling in his grave.

Blackadder. The first series of *Blackadder* used a lot more film than series two, which was studio-bound. The first episode, *The Foretelling*, sets up an alternative history that is pushed to the background a bit in the subsequent episodes. It has much of the university skit about it. It plays cleverly with history:

Painter: History has known many great liars. Copernicus, Goebbels, St Ralph the Liar [he is shown holding a sign which reads 'St Benedict the Liar'] but there have been none quite so vile as the Tudor King Henry VII. It was he who rewrote history to portray his precursor Richard III as a deformed maniac who killed his nephews in the Tower. But the real truth is that Richard was a kind and thoughtful man who cherished his young wards ... . As for who really killed Richard III and how the defeated Henry Tudor escaped with his life, all is revealed in this, the first chapter of a history never before told: the history of The Blackadder!

113

It sets up its alternative history with great authority. This is the world of the story. Richard Curtis specializes in creating imaginary worlds, worlds which never existed, where his comedy can flourish. Both the film *Notting Hill* and the TV series *The Vicar of Dibley* show us worlds that, though they have aspects of the real world, are strangely unreal. To a very large extent they make the comedy work.

As well as playing with history, *Blackadder* parodies Shakespeare knowingly. An example of this is the very funny coda that you only get if you get the Macbeth reference. The three witches mistake Edmund for Henry Tudor and tell him he will be King. After the credits, they realize their mistake.

> GONERIL
> He wasn't as I expected him.
>
> REGAN
> I thought he was very rude.
>
> GONERIL
> I thought Henry Tudor would be better looking.
>
> CORDELIA
> Yes – not so Jewish.
>
> REGAN
> ... more like that man who rode by just before.
>
> CORDELIA
> Oops.
>
> REGAN
> Oops.
>
> GONERIL
> Oops.
>
> REGAN
> We've done it again ...
>
> CORDELIA
> Silly witching ...

Episode one, *The Foretelling*, sets up the historically authentic but completely false world into which the basic characters Edmund, Baldrick and Percy tumble. Here they are introduced with many of their soon to be familiar traits and comedic riffs. It is Richard III's banquet before the battle of Bosworth.

> Cut to Edmund's end of the Royal banqueting table.
> Edmund gives a little wave back to the King; he turns to
> Percy, Duke of Northumberland.

EDMUND

Ah, Percy, you see how the King picks me out for special greeting?

PERCY

No, My Lord ...

A servant pokes his head in, refilling their goblets.

BALDRICK

I saw it, My Lord.

EDMUND

Ah, and what is your name, little fellow?

BALDRICK

My name is Baldrick, My Lord.

EDMUND

Ah. Then I shall call you ... 'Baldrick'!

BALDRICK

... and I shall call you 'My Lord', My Lord.

EDMUND

Mmmm ... I like the cut of your jib, young fellow m'lad! How would you like to be my squire in the battle to-morrow?

Baldrick kneels instantly. Percy trying to show off in front of Baldrick, speaks to Edmund.

PERCY

It will be a great day to-morrow for we nobles.

EDMUND

Well, not if we lose, Percy. If we lose, I'll be chopped to pieces. My arms will end up at Essex, my torso in Norfolk, and my genitalia stuck up a tree somewhere in Rutland.

BALDRICK

With you at the helm, My Lord, we cannot lose.

PERCY

(still trying to show off.) Well, we could if we wanted to!

EDMUND

Ah, but we won't, Percy, and I shall prove to all that I am a man!

PERCY

But you are a man, My Lord.

> EDMUND
> But how shall it be proved, Percy ...?
>
> PERCY
> Well, they could look up that tree in Rutland.
> (Edmund hits him.) My Lord!

The audience needed to learn the world of the story. In the first series of *Blackadder* they have some help from location-shooting and the use of special effects – a headless ghost, for example. But what the audience really learns about is the main characters. At the end of series one, everybody dies and you would not think that that augurs particularly well for re-commissioning. However, they are resurrected in series two at the court of Elizabeth I, now on videotape and confined to a few studio sets. But the freedom of the characters with history, a kind of knowing disregard, and their mutually dependent relationships remain intact.

Comedy often works by characters banging up against the walls of their world. *Fawlty Towers* is a very good example of this. What the audience had learned at the end of series one of *Blackadder*, was not so much the setting, the alternative history, but Edmund, Percy and Baldrick. So, when the walls closed in in season two, rather than weaken this relationship, it strengthened it. Like Fletcher, it actually helped that they were confined. The comedy is more focused – Edmund becomes more crafty, as Baldrick becomes more stupid and Percy reaches hysterical heights of idiocy. So the lesson we should learn from Blackadder is: however strange the rules of your world, make them clear and make sure that you and your characters respect them.

Character

British comedy is often about losers, whereas American comedy is nearly always aspirational. Characters like Hancock, Harold Steptoe and David Brent are fundamentally tragic. The gap between what they wish they were, what they think they are, what the world shows them to be, is the killing ground of laughter. As reality TV raises the bar, our appetite for watching the comedy of embarrassment seems to increase. David's Brent's famous dance seems to lead on to the concept of extras where Andy Millman's (Gervais) abject career sets up the guest stars who fall over themselves to parody their image in the interests of comedy. Millman's very failure critiques our celebrity-obsessed age. In the same way, Ricky Gervais's unique ability to make Jonathan Ross blush, critiques the whole idea of his chat show. The British can often be comfortable with failure, prepared to laugh at and with it, as in *Rab C. Nesbitt* by Ian Pattison, in a way the Americans cannot. The characters in *Friends* may, as somebody once remarked, behave 'like five old Jews in Miami' but they are glossy and beautiful people with boyfriends and girlfriends and exceptionally good hair.

Steptoe and Son. Writers Galton and Simpson first created the characters of Albert and Harold Steptoe, the father and son rag and bone men, in a single comedy playhouse called *The Offer*. The eventual series ran for twelve years.

Much of the comedy in Steptoe comes from pushing a realistic, potentially tragic situation, over the top, as in this extract from *The Desperate Hours*:

> ALBERT
> It's nice of you to stay home and keep me company, Harold.
>
> HAROLD
> I can't afford to go out anywhere, can I? I'm warning you, Dad, if we have another week like this, I'm turning it in. Thirty bob I've made this week. It's cost more than that to run the horse.
>
> ALBERT
> Oh don't worry, something'll turn up.
>
> HAROLD
> Yeah, my toes if we have much more of it. Three weeks it's been like this. All the savings have gone. The money we've got for pawning the television has gone, and the radio keeps going on and off when it feels like it. We've got a pile of bills over there we could paper the room with.
>
> ALBERT
> We could always burn them, get a bit of heat.
>
> HAROLD
> Well, they're not going to get paid, that's for sure. There's no decent grub in the house. My guts have been rumbling all day. Do you know what I've had to eat today? Half a carrot, and I had a fight to get that out of the horse's mouth. That old bird nearly whacked me with her umbrella. 'That's for the horse,' she said. (Pause) I've started getting hallucinations. You turned into a chicken ten minutes ago.
>
> ALBERT
> Stop exaggerating.
>
> HAROLD
> You don't know how close it was. If we'd had some stuffing handy it could have been very painful.

The situation of Harold tied to a father who perpetually stops him getting out, or indeed getting laid, remains the dynamic of the series. Wilfred Brambell (Albert) and Harry H. Corbett (Harold) were serious actors and played the truth of this almost Strindbergian relationship without flinching. It is not that all clowns want to play Hamlet but that Hamlet, a tragic figure, is always a potential clown. Shakespeare never forgets this. Famously In *Lear*, who is the clown – the King or the Fool? Good comic writers never lose sight of the seriousness of their heroes' and heroines' predicament. The more seriously they take it, the funnier it is.

Steptoe and Son was hysterically funny but it never short-changed its audience by soft-pedalling the destructive nature of the father and son relationship. Albert always dragged Harold back to him and mercilessly derided and demolished his every dream as in this extract from *The Desperate Hours*:

> ALBERT
>
> I ain't no crook.
>
> HAROLD
>
> You're worse. You're a ponce. You've been sucking the life blood out of me for years. Dracula would have been a better father than you. At least he only had a go at night, you're at it all day long. I've never had a chance.
>
> ALBERT
>
> Never had a chance – what could you have been?
>
> HAROLD
>
> Anything. I've got brains. I've just never had a chance to use them. I wanted to be a doctor, he wouldn't let me.
>
> ALBERT
>
> Well, that's saved a few lives, ain't it?

He continuously drives Harold almost to the point of violence and just when he is ready to walk out the door draws him back with his weakness. In another context we might recognize the truth, the underlying reality of this situation, and cry but in Steptoe it is always pushed to laughter.

Look at other comic characters, such as Rab C. Nesbitt, Alf Garnet or the extraordinary Sue White, the Staff Liaison Officer in *Green Wing* played by Michelle Gomez. Behind the comedy, what does she tell us about the character and the science of personnel management?

So, with reference to character we should learn: never deny the underlying truth of your characters.

> HUD HASTINGS
>
> Oooohhhhhhhhhh!
>
> GIANT REID
>
> Oooooooohhhhhhhhhhhh!

                    HUD HASTINGS
Oooohhhhhhhhhh!

                    GIANT REID
Oooohhhhooohhhh!

                    HUD HASTINGS
Ooooooohhhhhhhhhhhhh!

                    GIANT REID
Oooohhhhhhhhhh!

                    HUD HASTINGS
Oooohhhhhhhhhh!

                    GIANT REID
Oooohhhhhhhhhh!

                    HUD HASTINGS
Oooohhhhhhhhhh!

                    GIANT REID
Oooohhhhhhhhhh!

Comedy dialogue is like no other. Here is the opening exchange in series three, episode two of *Father Ted* by Graham Linehan and Arthur Matthews, *Chirpy Birpy Cheap Sheep*. Father Ted has bet the whole winter fuel allowance on the favourite sheep, Chris, in The King of The Sheep '98 competition that is shortly to be held on Craggy Island, but a strange beast is stalking the island.

                    FARGO
An' if he doesn't win, what does that mean Father?

                    TED
Well we won't have any heating. But if the rest of the year stays as warm as the summer, we're laughing. Come on, it's Chris. He's the champ. Talk about a safe bet!

                    HUD HASTINGS
Giant, have you heard about this creature going around terrorising sheep on the island?

                    GIANT REID
No. Tell me more.

                    HUD HASTINGS
They say it's as big as a jaguar.

                    GIANT REID
The car?

> HUD HASTINGS
> No. The big cat thing. And it's face is all teeth. Big
> white teeth as sharp as knives.
>
> GIANT REID
> Has it killed yet?
>
> HUD HASTINGS
> No, but it's only a matter of time.
>
> GIANT REID
> Hope it doesn't get any of my sheep.
>
> HUD HASTINGS
> No man's sheep is safe.
>
> GIANT REID
> Oh dear!
>
> HUD HASTINGS
> Oooohhhhhhhhhh! Etc ...

Dialogue

In Chapter 5, I talked about vernacular and argot. These are both very clear in Father Ted. The characters are Irish priests so the vernacular, the rhythm and pitch of the dialogue, is their Irish accents, as above when Ted is talking with some of his parishioners. The argot is that of the Catholic faith of which Ted, among his fellow priests, has a pretty firm grasp. He seems, off-stage at least, to perform his priestly functions, saying mass and the like; he knows what they are and what he should be. The wonderfully stupid Dougal, of course, has barely any idea of what a priest is or what he should believe.

> DOUGAL
> This resurrection thing (making face) what's that
> about?

The dynamic of their relationship is that, however daft Ted is, Dougal is dafter. This dynamic sings in their dialogue.

> Ted is reading a newspaper on the sofa of the parochial
> house. In the background is the sound of birds singing.
> Dougal is sitting at the table reading the back of a record
> sleeve – BBC Sound Effects Vo. 4. Dougal gets up to change
> the sound. The birds stop singing. Ted turns the newspaper
> page and drums sound. Ted coughs and the sound effect
> changes to gunfire.
>
> TED
> Dougal, give the album a rest now.

DOUGAL
Ah come on Ted it's brilliant. I think people will
soon give up listening to pop music and listen to
this type of thing instead.

TED
You know, from what I hear in the charts today
I'm not sure if that's not happening already.

DOUGAL
What? This is so good though Ted isn't it? They've
got all kinds of things. As if by magic I can create
a big crowd of invisible ducks. (Dougal plays a
sound of a train.) Or take you on a trip into darkest
Africa. (Dougal plays a sound of a toilet flushing.)
Or bring you into a spooky castle on a stormy night.
(The telephone rings.)

DOUGAL
Ooooooohhhhhh! Ooooooooooooohhhhhhhhhhh!

Mrs Doyle, their tea-obsessed housekeeper, comes in.
Here the vernacular is particularly strong.

TED
Mrs Doyle, are you alright? You look terrible,
doesn't she Dougal?

DOUGAL
Awful Ted!

MRS DOYLE
I didn't get much sleep, Father. I kept thinking
I heard this terrible howling noise.

DOUGAL
Oh that'd be the beast.

TED
What's this now?

MRS DOYLE
There's something terrible on the moors, Father.

Dougal plays an eerie sound effect.

TED
Moors? We don't have any moors.

MRS DOYLE
Well then there's something terrible roaming
around the place where normally there would

121

be moors Father. They think it might be a kind
of giant fox.

Dougal plays a thunder and lightning sound effect.

> TED
> Dougal!

The lesson here is that what a character says may not be true. Indeed
on Craggy Island it may be barely sane, but it is true to Ted, Dougal and
Mrs Doyle.

Another good example of vernacular is in the tirade, a frequent tool of
comic dialogue. Here is Alf Garnett in full flow in a speech from *Till Death Us
Do Part* by Johnnie Speight, another writer who wrote in longhand.

> ALF
> Listen, that woman, that Mary Whitehouse is
> concerned for the moral fibres and the well-being
> of this beloved country. (Mike blows a raspberry.)
> Never mind your [raspberry] that's being rotted away
> by your corrupt films and your telly and your bloody
> BBC's the worst of the lot with its *Top of The Pops*,
> and the evil painted youths dressed up as girls and
> that middle-aged peroxide-albino clunk click ponce
> they've got in charge of it.

> ELSE
> (mildly) I like it.

> ALF
> Yeah you bloody would wouldn't you. And and and
> and that seductive music and their singing about
> men's things. (Pause) And driving the youth of the
> country to crime and and and mugging and where's
> my bloody pipe. (Searching noisily) And bestialities
> of rape and and living like bloody gypsies and refusing
> to go to work and and bloody living off the dole and
> and and having no respect and mocking their elders
> and betters and calling me bloody skinhead!

Alf's tirades became a trademark and notably upset Mary Whitehouse, the
campaigner to clean up television, and politicians of all parties. Yet however
bravura, however much Speight revelled in the language, they were always
true to Alf's character. His bigotry and blinkered view of the world was as
consistent as the word Blackpool in a stick of rock.

Your dialogue should remain true to your character and to his or her
vernacular and argot.

Structure

When discussing *Porridge* and *Blackadder* we talked about containing comedy in cartoons and radio but comedy can have an epic quality. *Old Harry's Game*, a radio sitcom by Andy Hamilton, has the vast canvas of hell.

Let's examine the plot of an episode of *The Simpsons*.

Cape Feare written by Jon Vitti and directed by Rich Moore (first broadcast in USA 7 October 1993).

1. Sideshow Bob writes threatening note to Bart from prison. Bart and Family are frightened.

2. Sideshow Bob is paroled and attends cinema, where he threatens Simpsons.

3. The FBI relocate them in a witness protection to Lake Feare.

4. They drive off. Homer has not told Grandpa. He can't get into their old house to get his medication.

5. Homer drives them to Lake Feare, unaware that Sideshow Bob is clinging to the underside of their car. They all sing along to a tape of the FBI chorus singing Gilbert and Sullivan selections. Homer playfully drives through cactus causing Sideshow Bob much pain.

6. They settle into a houseboat. Sideshow Bob swims aboard, ties up family and chases Bart with a knife.

7. Art seems doomed but, appealing to Sideshow Bob's vanity, he gets him to sing the whole of HMS Pinafore while the boat drifts upstream.

8. Just in the nick of time, as Sideshow Bob takes his bow. The boat runs aground next to a brothel where, luckily, the Springfield police force are being entertained. The cops manage to arrest Sideshow Bob.

9. Coda. The Simpsons return home. Grandpa, unable to get at his medication, has changed into a woman. Marge urges them to hurry but Granpa wants to delay as an old guy has offered to date him.

There is a great deal of plot crammed into this 22-minute episode. It comprises not only a parody of Martin Scorsese's *Cape Fear* (1991) but an examination of the Simpson family under pressure. It includes Bart's resourcefulness, Marge's misgivings and Homer's ability to go along with anything. It contains slapstick sight gags like Sideshow Bob being dragged through the cactus and, when he crawls out from under the car, a succession of rakes that, as he steps on them, bang him in the face. It also has the wonderful comic idea of an FBI chorus singing operetta. This I feel is so strange it must be true. It covers a lot of territory geographically. There are scenes on land and water.

The writer may be tempted to say that this is only possible because it is a cartoon but examine the economy with which this quite complex story is told. There is not an ounce of fat on it. Every line is made to count and every image to move the story along. Can this be said of your script? Ask yourself this question.

Another sort of comedy structure worth examining is in Larry David's *Curb Your Enthusiasm*. This show is largely improvised. The scenes are shot with two cameras to maintain continuity, at least within the individual takes. The cast often take flight to great comic effect. However, this spontaneity belies a very careful structure. There is a script, and the plotting is detailed and never sloppy. Things happen for a reason and the scenes, however spontaneous, are always set within that structure, so that each scene moves the plot along. Here is a step sheet for series five of *Curb Your Enthusiasm*, episode five, *Lewis Needs a Kidney*.

1. Larry rings Jones Security – PI Jones is trying to find Larry's real parents. Larry in a previous episode learned he was adopted. The receptionist won't put him through till he says what it is regarding. He won't, he pisses her off and slams down the phone.

2. Larry locks himself out of his car outside the Jack in The Box restaurant. He rings Jeff. Jeff says he'll come. The restaurant is closed but the Drive Thru is open. Larry stands behind the queuing cars. He moves forward but they won't serve him because he's not in a car. A motorist Pete takes pity on him. Larry remarks on Pete's porn collection in the back of the car. Pete's vague about what he does. Jeff arrives, they all eat Jumbo Jacks and Larry learns that Lewis needs a kidney.

3. Leo's deli. Lewis is even more down than usual. There are no kidney donors. His useless cousin Louis Lewis, who works at Jack in the Box, won't donate an organ till he is dead. If only a buddy would come through. He looks pleadingly at Larry. Larry is silent.

4. That evening Larry tells Cheryl that he must choose healthier friends. He says he can't deal with it and what's more, at the first sign of illness, Cheryl is out too. He says he'll take the test. She says he's a very sweet man. She hugs him. His hand slides to her ass. She rebukes him for trying to turn consolation into sex. Snuggle, no sex.

5. Larry on the phone to Richard, Lewis's assistant. She asks what it's regarding. Mindful of the other receptionist in beat 1, Larry says it is about Lewis's kidney transplant. This is the first the assistant has heard of it. She becomes hysterical.

6. Richard Lewis comes round. He has a go at Larry about upsetting his assistant. Larry tells him he will take the test. The police ring.

7. At the police station Larry tries to persuade Jeff to take the test. Mr Jones arrives. He has a go at Larry about upsetting his receptionist. The identity parade, Jeff says he will take the test. They both identify number 2 as the Pete who they had dinner with. The detective is pissed that they have given an alibi to Peter Hagan who has a string of aliases and is a known criminal.

8. Larry and Jeff take the test. The nurse says good news, both their blood types match. She and Jeff have a routine.

9. In the Park, Larry and Jeff discuss how they will decide who donates. Larry suggests Bingo at which he is very skilled. Jeff says, no way. They agree to let Lewis decide, and that neither is to campaign to influence the decision.

10. Larry in Lewis's office. Lewis's secretary weeps. Larry consoles her. He strokes her hair. She freaks and, accusing him of coming on to her, leaves. Lewis is furious, says he doesn't care how Jeff and Larry decide. Flip a coin! He exits calling Larry a Wack Job.

11. At Jeff's house, Marty Funkhouser (Bob Einstein) prepares to flip a coin. He thinks it's a beautiful thing they are doing but won't take the test himself. They do 'eeeny meeny miney mo' and Larry loses. They argue about the decision. Susie enters and tells Jeff that he's not donating any fucking kidneys to anyone. Larry exits disconsolate, coming back to collect his coin.

12. Larry protests the rules of Eeny Meeny. Cheryl says they got it right. Larry is it. Cheryl says maybe God saved Larry from drowning for this noble act. She consoles him and again is turned off when Larry's hand squeezes her ass. However on TV they see that Peter Hagan has been arrested for robbing Jumping Jack's Drive Thru Restaurant. In the robbery, Louis Lewis (Lewis's cousin) has been shot. He is in a coma and not expected to survive. Larry jumps for joy! Freeze Frame.

The moral dilemna is: do you give up a kidney to save a friend? In Larry's case, while he wishes to be noble, his nobility is perpetually sabotaged by Lewis's reactions and his own cowardice.

Beat 10. Let's examine beat 10 in the step sheet. Both Larry and Jeff have the right blood type so they have to decide which of them will donate a kidney to Louis. Larry goes to Lewis's office. The scene that Larry hopes will be about Lewis feeling grateful that Larry is prepared to offer his kidney becomes instead about Lewis's assistant accusing Larry of coming on to her. Here you can see that an improvised scene has been set up with two agendas for Larry. He wants to tell Lewis that he will make this supreme gesture of friendship. He wants to comfort the assistant. However, while hugging her, he strokes her hair and this freaks her out. Larry's instinct to turn a hug into a caress has already been set up with Cheryl, his wife, in beat 4. The scene ends with the assistant quitting and Lewis storming out. Saying he doesn't care how Larry and Jeff decide who gives the kidney. Flip a coin! He leaves calling Larry a wack job.

The dialogue in this scene is improvised, but the parameters are not. Larry must go from nobility to derision. Louis must go from gratitude to anger. The assistant must go from sadness to outrage. When you write a scene it is useful to think about beat 10. Does each of your characters make a journey within the scene? Do they have enough ammunition in their motivation (sadness/anger, self-satisfaction/humiliation), to interact dynamically with the plot? A good scene will generally have at least two elements in it, two agendas for the characters. A good scene will always move the plot along.

Get the DVD of series five and look at *Lewis Needs A Kidney* with the step sheet above. Note how the plot is structured in such a way as to give the improvised scenes a richness. Note how, as with the Simpson's episode, there is no fat on the story. Everything moves the plot along. Note too how the episode makes furious fun of something very serious.

Do not let the form (the slot or the genre) limit the richness and detail of your individual scenes and plot.

Time

Time in the world of comedy could perhaps best be measured in laughs. The comedian on stage, if he or she is not getting laughs, knows time lasts forever. Your comedy script, if it doesn't cause laughter, will seem interminable. Above I have talked about how comedy often works best when it is confined within four or at least three walls. This allows the characters to bounce off the walls of their world to comic effect. *The Royle Family* by Caroline Aherne and Craig Cash (series one and three), Aherne, Henry Normal and Carmel Morgan (series two) have all the qualities mentioned above. Witty dialogue, strong characters, a contained setting and a basic truth about those characters drawn from the Northern working-class backgrounds of the writers.

If comedy is tilting the mirror to show us ourselves, then *The Royle Family* is the prime example. As we all know the world of *The Office*, we all know the situation of the Royles, slumped on their couch and watching an unseen television. In this comedy, the fourth wall is us. Now you may protest that your television watching, like mine, is sensitive, critical and informed! I respond like Jim – my arse.

Like those people who maintain they never watch television, just before they outline a programme they have seen recently. The Royle family do very little but as they talk their lives are revealed. Mostly they are in real time and a lot of the time they are bored, so their time stretches out. Our time flies by because they are funny and they involve us. So their clock, the clock of the characters, may drag on but it allows us to look at them closely.

One of the things that UK television has always done is to make us look at people who are often disregarded. From the *Boys from the Black Stuff* to *Shameless*, working-class characters without a voice have been given a voice. Caroline Aherne and her co-writers, by removing all the props that are supposed to make drama interesting, forces the audience to look at something that we might normally pass by. This is one of the most important functions of art.

In *The Royle Family*, simple things like eating chocolates can pass in real time, drawing us into their world. Bickering, obscenities, stupid fights about nothing, can reveal both humour and pain. Because we are made to share the clock of these characters, in some sense share their tedium; we are drawn into their world. In the end it achieves the true purpose of drama. In the end, we care.

So what can we learn from this? That the time of your characters has to be respected. That excitement is not dynamic camera moves and exploding cars but people.

> If you can make your audience share the clock of your characters, you can get them to reveal themselves to the audience. You can slow your audience down so they have to look.

Checklist

So, the five lessons from comedy are:

1. However strange the rules of your world, make them clear and make sure that you and your characters respect them.
2. Never deny the underlying truth of your characters.
3. Your dialogue should remain true to your character and to his or her vernacular and argot.
4. A good scene will generally have at least two elements in it, two agendas for the characters. A good scene will always move the plot along.
5. If you can make your audience share the clock of your characters, you can get them to reveal themselves to the audience. You can slow your audience down so they have to look.

CODA

On all journeys you learn something. In this book I have taken you on a journey through a selection of creative TV writing. The purpose of the journey is to learn something about the craft. The shows we have looked at in the various chapters under the headings of pilot, character, dialogue, structure and time, will I hope provide you with the inspiration to examine other shows yourself. Using these chapters as a model, you should be able to approach any kind of TV drama and understand what makes it tick. Using the same methods you can break down your own writing and understand other writers' work and stories when you collaborate.

The various formats for TV drama are under constant death sentence, and since I began working in it, TV drama itself has regularly been pronounced dead. 'The sitcom is dead, the sketch show is dead, the drama documentary is dead!' TV is a necropolis of formats but, turn your back, and the dead zombies rise up with encouraging regularity. All these formats need writers.

Your ability to work in the shifting sands of television must be based on a clear-eyed understanding of what is currently happening with TV. This you can get by watching it critically and studying the media supplements of the papers. The caveat is that the medium is riddled with gossip and paranoia, and often the financial pages tell you more than the arts pages. Also, the most reliable guide to what is happening behind the scenes is what actually appears on the box. It does take time for a TV show to be made and to air, but this time-lag is constantly shrinking; this is because most productions are made on borrowed money that only gets repaid when the show is broadcast.

The TV writer should also try and guard some corner of his or her creativity that is not subject to the will o' the wisp nature of the medium. This is very hard to do, for most writers put their all into what they write, but it can be useful when, for no fault of your own, you find yourself shown the door.

The best writers often have such an inviolable core. Mere fashion will never destroy Jimmy McGovern's fractured Catholic creativity. Nor Paul Abbott's strong sense of where he comes from and the worth of the characters he has met and those he creates.

Recently, reality shows and the popular melodrama of soaps, combined with the tabloid noise around their stars, have created a culture where drama has felt it must shout to be heard. Yet the strong individual voices of the two writers above consistently punch through the noise and hook their audiences, because this is not writing by numbers but writing from the heart – creative TV writing.

McGovern and Abbott came up through the soaps, Brookside and Coronation Street, respectively. Russell T. Davies, the third in the current trinity of top UK TV writers, wrote initially for the afternoon children's TV series *Children's Ward.*

There was a time when, much as British actors despised film acting, British writers rather despised soap writing. The example of these three writers should tell us that in no way is this position tenable. Nobody becomes a worse writer by writing. Years of neglect and rejection can sap your will to continue but if you keep writing, and if you or others examine what you write critically, then you will continue to grow as a writer. If you nurture your curiosity about the world, and discipline that curiosity in the ways I have discussed in Chapter 1, then the well of your creativity will not run dry.

In so far as we can be certain about anything, we can be certain that time-based broadcasts will become less and less important. People will programme from their laptops, hard disc recorders or mobile phones, the shows they want to watch. They will be able to watch these on the move if they wish. This will mean that loyalty to a show or a writer is much easier to sustain. It also means that through download to own, the ability to download a file down the phone line and other technological advances it will be much easier to catch that episode in season two of *The Sopranos* that you missed. Leaving aside piracy, which gets easier by the day, we will legitimately be able to dial up anything we want. I already do this with the three writers above. I never miss their work because I know that, even if I don't like it, it will be worth my time.

Time of course remains the most precious commodity in the twenty-first century. We are constantly being sold the idea that technology is saving us time. We start work with laptop and mobile phone as soon as we get on the train in the morning little realizing that technology has actually robbed us of a chunk of free time. It has moved the office into our home and extended our working day. Fine if you enjoy your work, not so good if you hate it.

There is a paradox at the heart of television. It is the most modern and yet also the most conservative medium. Because we allowed it into our homes, it was heavily censored and often timid in its conception. Much of broadcast television has allowed itself to be boxed into uncreative slots by the genre police. It is often being broken down in ways that appear revolutionary, only to turn out to be fundamentally glossy ways of maintaining the status quo – in the same way that laddism was sold as liberation (no-inhibitions no political correctness) but was in fact a clever way of chaining a segment of consumers more securely to the market.

The TV writer should always embrace technology but should realize that what they have to offer the medium is not technological, it is the creativity in their brains that can be unlocked with a felt tip or a quill pen.

When I teach acting for the camera. I start the drama students with a cruel but simple exercise. They film themselves speaking a Shakespeare sonnet into the digital camera. Holding the camera, like Hamlet, in what I call the 'Yorick position'. The modern camera is no heavier than a Jester's skull. This exercise does two things: firstly it confronts straight away any natural insecurities the young actors may have about the way they look; these can then be faced up to right away in the clear knowledge that any other camera position is going to make them look better. Secondly – and this is what is relevant to the TV writer – something strange happens when Shakespeare's sonnets are acted into a camera. Sonnets were written by one person for another to read. They were not like plays, where several actors performed loudly before an audience. They were private and intimate. Often intended only for the eyes and ears of a lover or friend. The camera understands this. It replays them to you as freshly as they would have been when their first Elizabethan reader broke the seal on the original letter that contained them. Try it sometime, because that bond between the written word, the individual imagination of the writer, and the intricacies of Sony electronics is where the strength of creative TV writing resides.

APPENDIX STEP OUTLINE OF *THE SHIELD*

EPISODE 4 *DAWG DAYS* (WRITTEN BY KEVIN ARKADIE. DIRECTOR: STEPHEN GYLLENHAAL)

1. *The Shake Club.*

Officer Danielle Sofer and Lieutenant Curtis ('Lemonhead') Lemansky are moonlighting as security at the Shake Club, a rap and soul venue. Rapper Kern Little takes the stage with his beautiful protégé Tyesha – whereupon there's a commotion as rival rapper T-Bonz and his crew burst into the club. T-Bonz demands money he claims Kern owes him. Danielle and Lewansky try to cool things out, but insults start to fly and a shootout ensues.

2. *'Two dead, six wounded.'*

Detective 'Dutch' Wagenbach, Detective Vic Mackey and Captain Aceveda arrive on the scene. Aceveda wants to know if there are any suspects already in custody. The shooter is identified – one Rondell Robinson, one of Mackey's drug-dealers. Mackey retorts that the night is young – he'll take care of it. The two men clash over how to handle the investigation and their respective areas of jurisdiction.

3. *'Stand down their armies.'*

Danielle Sofer tells Aceveda she can identify the lethal shooter at the club. Wagenbach, Lewansky and Mackey confer. The prime danger is that this feud will spill out onto the streets. The problem: how to get T-Bonz and Kern to stand down their armies.

4. *'I'm just backing up my boy.'*

Mackey and Lewansky go to Rondell Robinson's apartment, which is stuffed with expensive hi-fi equipment. We learn that Kern – a long-time buddy of Rondell's – financed Rondell's entry into the dope trade. Rondell tells Mackey that T-Bonz used to be on Kern's record label. The two then parted. Kern made a lot of money on his own, but T-Bonz feels he's been cut out of the loop and is entitled to a share; whence the dispute. It also transpires that Rondell is one of Mackey's network of dealers – tolerated as long as there's no aggravation and they pay their dues. Mackey tells Rondell to keep his dealers off the streets – no targets out there. Meanwhile he wants to set up a meeting with Kern

Little, and demands that Rondell name two of the shooters at the club, who are duly brought into the precinct.

5. *'I sometimes have ulterior motives.'*
Aceveda and his wife, Aurora, attend the inauguration of a new housing project attended by prominent members of the Hispanic community. Aceveda is eager to meet the man behind the project, the influential Jorge Machado. Machado tells Aceveda that his nanny's husband Manuel Ruiz is missing – not an unusual occurrence, but this time his wife is worried. He's a casual worker, working out of the home improvement centre. The nanny's upset, therefore his wife is upset. Can Aceveda help? From the exchange, we gather a quid pro quo is definitely on the cards ...

6. *'Give the word to your crew; the war's over!'*
Mackey and Lewanksy come calling on Kern at a studio in Bel Air where Tyesha is recording her latest album. Kern insists that when the shooting started he grabbed Tyesha and made for the exit. Tyesha comes in, cuddling her dog Wacko. She tells Mackey that Kern isn't behind the war – his boys opened fire to defend him. Kern tells Mackey he'll handle T-Bonz – he's nothing if not a man of peace.

7. *'I can't believe we're doing this for some fat cat's nanny.'*
The precinct. Aceveda brings Mrs Ellie Ruiz in and assigns Wagenbach to her case, partnered with Detective Claudette Wyms. Wagenbach is pissed off at being hauled off the high-profile Shake Club case.

8. *'Yo no se ...'*
At the home improvement centre – a casual labour depot – Claudette Wymas and Wagenbach question migrant workers about Manuel and locate someone who has a tale to tell.

9. *'Nothing's for free!'*
Mackey and Lewanksy intercept two of of Rondell's dope runners. What are they doing out on the street? Incensed, Mackey storms into Rondell's apartment, browbeats Rondell into doing as he's told on pain of having his dope 'franchise' terminated.

10. *'They used to be best friends ...'*
Claudette Wyms and Dutch Wagenbach bring Aceveda news. The word is that Manuel had an altercation with one Eduardo Salcido aboard the truck that brought them into California. Apparently the two of them grew up together in Mexico. The agenda: find Salcido. They were both working for a trucking warehouse, Jamison Contracting.

11. *'If I can't defend you, I can't afford you.'*
On the move, Mackey and Lewansky pick up a call. There has been a multiple shooting – the rappers' private war has gone public. They arrive at the scene to find a blood-bath with four fatalities, and a small boy who has come to grief under the wheels of a gang member's car. Assistant Chief Ben Gilroy arrives on the scene and takes Mackey aside. The mayor knows the boy's family, so

he's taking a personal interest in this. Gilroy is displeased that, having sanctioned the Strike Team and its unusual approach to policing, it doesn't appear to be doing its job. Vendrell brings news: The kid was DOA.

14.40

Act 2

12. *'This war ends here!'*

Mackey has convened a meet between T-Bonz and Kern. T-Bonz insists that Kern stole Tyesha from him – he was her lover and musical mentor. It was T-Bonz who coached Tyesha when she made her first CD, so Kern owes T-Bonz $2 million. Kern retorts that when she was with T-Bonz, she wasn't selling any records. He offers a deal, which T-Bonz rejects. Mackey tells him to go away and come back with some numbers, and T-Bonz to cool it. Otherwise he'll throw them both in jail. There is to be a 24-hour ceasefire. Anyone breaks it, they're for it.

13. *Eduardo Salcido.*

Claudette Wyms and Dutch Wagenbach go to the Jamison Company Yard where renovations are being carried out by migrant construction workers. Jamison knows Manuel, but tells the cops he worked for a day and then never returned. The two cops go looking for Eduardo, who escapes.

14. *'The jury is going to love her ...'*

Aceveda reviews the list of suspects for the Shake Club shooting and singles out Rondell Robinson. He tells Rondell he has a witness who will i.d. him as the shooter – a cop. The jury will love her. And he cautions Rondell that if he imagines a corrupt policeman can protect him while he deals drugs and commits murder, he's sorely mistaken.

15. *'I'll handle Aceveda.'*

Mackey confers with Rondell, who reassures him that when Aceveda came to his apartment, no drugs were found. But Aceveda suspects he's being protected by a cop. Mackey says he'll handle Aceveda.

16. *'I could be of great use to you.'*

Aceveda updates Machado on Manuel Ruiz. They have a suspect, who won't be able to elude them for long. The quid pro quo – a seat is coming vacant on the city council, and Aceveda wants it. He'd then be in a position to do the Hispanic community – and Machado – a lot of good. Machado tells him he can't sell a cop to the voters the way things are. What about a cop who exposed corruption in the force? Could Machado sell him? Absolutely.

17. *'It's a crime, ain't it? Digging up my son?'*

Danielle Sofer and Officer Julien Lowe attend a call from a distraught black woman, Dottie Cummings, whose son Thurman's body has been dug up and held for ransom. Lowe stays with her ...

18. *'I've got a little problem.'*

As Danielle arrives back at the precinct, she's accosted by Mackey. Rondell Robinson is an informant of his. He was firing in self-defence at the club. Could

Danielle be persuaded to suffer from blurred recollections? Danielle says she'll think about it.

19. *'Henry? Is that you?'*

Back at Mrs Cummings's house, it transpires that Lowe went to high school with Thurman, who went on to become a hoodlum and was shot robbing a liquor store. The phone rings – the extortionist attempting to disguise his voice. The woman realizes who this is: Henry? Is that you?

20. *'I wanted to take my new lady on one of them cruises.'*

Henry proves to be a middle-aged black man, a former boyfriend of Mrs Cummings. He tells Lowe that he knew Dottie had life insurance. He wanted to take his new lady on a cruise. Lowe points out that Mrs Cummings spent the money on Thurman's funeral. Henry is crestfallen.

21. *'He thinks he's a dog, now.'*

Mackey has a dilemma at home. His son is showing behavioural problems, which Mackey won't acknowledge. He attempts to humour his wife.

22. *'Forget what you saw at the Shake Club!'*

Meanwhile Danielle is attacked in the street. A black man holds a gun to her head and tells her to forget what she saw at the Shake Club – or else.

23. *'You don't scare me ...'*

Danielle angrily confronts Rondell Robinson in the lock-up, tells him he can't intimidate her. Rondell denies everything, and remarks she does look pretty scared. Mackey witnesses the exchange and wants to know what's going on. Danielle asks him if he told Rondell it was she who i.d.'d him. Mackey denies this. He tells Danielle he'll take care of it. Danielle angrily retorts she can take care of herself.

24. *'Cops are off limits.'*

Mackey grabs Rondell by the throat. He's crossed the line by targeting a police officer. Mackey tells him to use his drug money to bail himself out. By the time the case gets to court, Mackey will have sabotaged it.

28.28

Act 3

25. *'He's got that look.'*

Wagenbach and Claudette Wyms track down Eduardo Salcido and interrogate him, while Aceveda observes. Eduardo won't say what happened on the truck. Wyms surmises that he was raped. She knows the look.

26. *'That goddam bastard's gotta pay!'*

Kern and Tyesha show up in Mackey's office with a cardboard box containing Wacko – stiff and cold, poisoned by T-Bonz. Tyesha demands that Kern do something, or she'll find a man who will. Mackey can feel the situation spinning out of control. Kern proposes that he pay Mackey to whack Kern – being a cop he can get to him. He'll pay double if he can watch. Mackey sees a way out of this. Gimme the address ...

27. *'He slipped ... and he fell.'*
Wyms and Wagenbach extract a confession from Eduardo ... but the 'killing' turns out to have been an accident. Manuel fell from the roof. But Jamison insisted it was murder.

28. *'This what you call planting rice and beans?'*
The Jamison Yard. Jamison turns up to find Manuel Ruiz's body being exhumed from the yard under Claudette Wyms's and Dutch's supervision. He had it buried there in order to avoid red-tape and keep the business running smoothly.

29. *'I'm never for sale!'*
Night. Mackey, accompanied by Lewansky, brings T-Bonz to a freight depot. T-Bonz remonstrates. You broke the truce, Mackey tells him. Kern is there, waiting for Mackey to shoot T-Bonz. Then the cops level their guns at both rappers. At first we think that Mackey and Lewansky are going to shoot Kern and T-Bonz, but they bundle them into a shipping container. You two don't make peace, I'll see one of you in the morning, Mackey tells them.

30. *'Maybe he's got a rich uncle.'*
The precinct. Aceveda remarks to Mackey that Rondell Robinson has posted $100k in bail. A lot of money for a ghetto kid. And Officer Lowe, aware that Danielle Sofer is troubled, tells her he'll pray for her that night.

31. *'You went after a cop, Rondell ...'*
He returns to his apartment to find Mackey and Lewansky there, and the place stripped bare. His expensive hi-fi and TV have been donated to a local boys' club, his beloved record collection trashed. Retribution. Lewansky consoles him. Mackey wanted to do a lot worse.

32. *'Mucho dinero.'*
Resolution of the Manuel Ruiz case. It was an accident. Jamison will be fined and released. But Mrs Ruiz will be able to sue his company for a lot of money.

33. *'Show me what you can do.'*
Machado tells Aceveda he'll consider backing him for the council elections. He'll be watching his performance with close interest.

34. *'What's next, Eduardo?'*
Eduardo is free to go. Wagenbach asks Eduardo his plans. He's got this wall at his place needs fixing ...

35. *'Do you trust me?'*
Mackey tells Danielle he's taken care of the threat to her. There's a frisson of romance between them. Then the phone rings ...

36. *'It's going to be OK ...'*
...summoning Mackey to the hospital. His 5-year-old son has bitten his baby sister, causing her to fall on her head. Mackey slumps down beside his son, who is strangely quiet. It's going to be OK ...

37. *'You hungry?'*

The freight yard, dawn. Mackey and Lewansky open the container. Kern emerges. T-Bonz is dead. Lewansky tells Mackey he'll dispose of the body. Mackey and Kern are left together.

41.56

End of episode 4.

Teaser:.1.00.

Total running time: 42.56.

GLOSSARY

Act One of the main divisions of a drama or film, completing a definite part of the action.

Antagonist (*see* Protagonist) The character who opposes the protagonist.

Arc As in story arc, character arc, the trajectory of a story, the moral and emotional journey a character makes through a story.

Back-story What has happened in a character's life before the start of the action.

Beat Term borrowed from music and applied to dramatic progression, used to describe a significant point in a passage of dialogue, a scene or a sequence. A beat can mark a shift in the character's actions or emotions. In terms of plot structure it can be a minor or a major turning-point.

Catharsis The purging of the emotions.

Character path Same as character arc above.

Chorus A grouping of characters who comment on the action.

Cliff From cliff-hanger. Something left unresolved that hopefully lures you the next episode.

Climax (from Greek for ladder.) A point in the plot where dramatic conflict reaches its highest point. The peak of the action in the drama, but not necessarily the end of the drama. Each will have at least one climax and probably many mini-climaxes.

Coda A passage added after the ending to form a more satisfactory conclusion to the piece. In the USA called 'a tag'.

Comedy (*see* Tragedy)

Conflict Actions resulting from physical, moral, or emotional antagonism between characters with differing objectives, or the inner struggle of a character.

Crisis The high point of physical, moral or emotional conflict, that precedes the climax.

Dénouement The un-knotting of the strands of the plot, for example the explanation of the clues in a detective story or the exposing of the misunderstandings in a Romcom, that lead up to the resolution of the drama.

Development The phase of a project extending from the initial idea to the start of pre-production, during which the script is commissioned and re-written and the producer raises finance. During this period, the producer (*see* below) proceeds to attract bankable talent to the project and obtain a deal with a broadcaster.

Drama (From Greek verb 'to do'.) A story related through dialogue and action.

Empathy Dramatic effect whereby the audience identifies with a character who may or may not be admirable.

Executive producer A catch-all term. He or she can be a writer, a broadcasting executive, a financier. An executive producer can be purely contractual or have editorial in-put and clout.

Finale The last movement in opera, musical theatre or film musicals in which the whole cast is assembled and sing together. In episodic TV drama the finale appears at the season's end.

Format In a TV drama the essential characters and their situation that create the shape that all the subsequent episodes follow.

Genre (From the French word for 'Kind'.) A type of film or drama; tragedy, comedy, thriller, musical, etc. Ultimately, the story-telling tradition to which the piece belongs.

High concept Audacious basic idea, An unusual or startling project with a high wow factor, e.g. *24.*

Inciting incident What happens to disturb the protagonist's world at the beginning of a drama.

Line producer The person who is responsible for the day-to-day operation of a television series or film and the logistics of production.

Log-line Originally the entry in the studio's log that answers the question: What is this project about? A brief pitch that encapsulates a film.

Montage Visual story-telling through a series of cuts, or the establishment of mood or locale through juxtaposition of images.

Narrative drive The momentum of a drama created by the application of story-telling techniques.

Objective What a character wants (*see* Super-objective).

On the nose Term used to denote dialogue or action that is over-explicit, i.e. lacking sub-text.

Pace The rate of dramatic progression.

Pathos The emotion generated by the spectacle of suffering.

Plot A conflict or series of conflicts unfolding in time.

Point of no return The point in the drama where a character is irrevocably committed to a course of action.

Problem That which the protagonist must act to solve – nail the killer, save the girl, oust a sexist boss, make right what is rotten in the State of Denmark.

Producer Finds the project, finds finance and continues to control the project editorially through production, delivery and sales.

Protagonist (lit: chief actor, character or combatant) Often used to denote the lead character, hero or heroine. Ultimately, those who act in a story.

Reversal Incident that causes a character to suffer an unforeseen set-back while s/he pursues her/his objective.

Scene A passage of continuous action in a particular setting or locale.

Screenplay Script stages and forms of which are:

1. Development. From the initial idea through to pre-production, where a shooting script has been completed.
2. Outline. A clear statement of the idea typically around two pages in length.
3. Step-outline. The story's structure in rigorous chronological sequence, often worked out by writing cards or post-it notes. Defines the progression of the story.
4. Treatment. A narrative version of the script, normally a sales document. A treatment should not normally exceed 25 pages in length.
5. First draft. The completed script before editing, revisions and rewriting of dialogue.
6. Synopsis. A summary of the story after the script has been completed.

Schedule The broadcast evening as shown in the TV guide.

Scheduling The art of designing this timetable.

Sequence A succession of scenes linked together by time, location, or continuous narrative forming a discrete episode or movement of a film.

Script editor Working alongside the writer to deliver the project to the broadcaster or producer. The writer's contact with the many voices with opinions on his or her script.

Scripturgy (neologism) From dramaturgy, the literature of the 'science' of writing scripts.

Show runner (Showrunner) Usually the lead writer or creator of the series, who often takes an executive producer credit, he or she is responsible for leading the writing team and overseeing the series editorially.

Slot The time allocated in the schedule for a drama to be transmitted.

Spine As in 'the spine is her losing her baby'. The main plotline that provides the backbone of an episode.

Step-outline The action of a film laid out in rigorous chronological sequence. Used in script development and for purposes of analysis. In USA this is called a beat sheet.

Storyliner Person who supervises the stories in a series.

Subplot A conflict developing in time, which is subsidiary to the main plot and which weaves into it. Often features secondary characters.

Sub-text The real conscious or unconscious intent behind what a character says or does. (*See* On the nose.)

Super-objective A scripturgical word meaning the ultimate goal of a character.

Suspense The need to know what is going to happen next and/or what will be the ultimate outcome of dramatic conflict or conflicts.

Suspension of disbelief The audience's willingness to succumb, for the purpose of being entertained and emotionally engaged, to the plausibility of a plot even if it defies logic.

Synopsis A brief or general statement of the theme and content of a film.

Tag (*see* Coda)

Teaser A short trailer for next week's episode played after the credits.

Tempo The distinctive rhythm of a film, play or TV drama.

Theme The subject-matter of a drama stated in terms of morality or the human condition.

Throughline The narrative line created by the protagonist's pursuit of his or her objective.

Tone The aesthetic quality and appeal of a TV drama, film or play.

Tragedy Tragedy focuses on the contradictions in human beings and in the human condition that make men and women the authors of their own destruction. Tragedy is a metaphor for life in time, which must end in death. It is about man negotiating with death. On the other hand, in comedy those contradictions are seen as something we have to live every day and wrestle with as best we can. Comedy is about instinct versus social constriction, appearance set against reality.

Treatment Presentation of a project in well-developed present-tense narrative form covering every event and all the major action in the proposed episode or series. A treatment is primarily a selling document.

Turning point A point in the story when a character is faced with a crucial decision.

Working title A temporary title assigned to a project during production and editing.

BIBLIOGRAPHY

It's easy to find books about TV and screenwriting, so here are some slightly more out of the way suggestions.

Critics
Aristotle *Poetics* (Hackett, translated by R. Janko).
The daddy of them all. Most criticism and all scripturgy, good and bad, stems from this work.
Cambell, J. *The Hero with a Thousand Faces* (Paladin).
Hugely influential book about myth.
Buckman, P. *All For Love – A Study in Soap Opera* (Secker and Warburg).
Authoritative book about soap opera now out of print, but libraries have it.
Friedmann, J. *How to Make Money Scriptwriting* (Boxtree).
Clear and unpretentious, full of excellent advice.
Shelley, J. *Interference* (Guardian Books).
Booker, C. *Screen Burn*.
Two witty and informed cristics who will take you on an entertaining ride through the last ten years of TV.
Brenton, S., Cohen, R. and Cohan, R. *Shooting People: Adventures in Reality TV*.
Good book about reality TV.

Writers On Writing
King, S. *On Writing*.
Need one say more.
Highsmith, P. *Plotting and Writing Suspense Fiction* (David and Charles). Now out of print.
A genius of suspense gives sound advice.
Elroy, J. *My Dark Places* (1877, Random House).
How the scars of experience are turned to fiction.
Sage, L. *Bad Blood*.
On how to write yourself whole.

Robinson, B. *The Peculiar Memories of Thomas Penman.*
Growing up to write.

On Directing
Katz, S.D. *Film Directing: Shot by Shot.*
An excellent book on the craft of directing.
Mackendrick, A. (ed. P.C. Faber) *On Film Making.*
A great director who was also a great teacher, full of good sense.
Mamet, D. *True and False.*
Good book about acting from a writer/director.

Reference
Black, A. and C. *Writers and Artists Year Book* (London).
Published every year all you need to know.
Flint, Fitzpatrick and Thorne. *A User's Guide to Copyright.*
Legal stuff but comprehensible by the layman.

Trade Papers and Magazines
Screen International
Scriptwriter
The Hollywood Reporter
Variety
Broadcast (the most relevant for TV)
MovieScope (see below for link)
http://www.thescreenwritersstore.net/product_info.php/cPath/67/
products_id/159

Websites
Bectu.org.uk (Broadcast Entertainment Cinematograph and Theatre Union).
Film council.org.uk
Pact.org.uk producers (Alliance for Cinema and TV in the UK).
Screendaily.comScreen International on-line
Screenwriters store.co.uk (Books, scripts software).
Jumptheshark.com
Uk.imdb.com (Internet movie database).
Variety.com (Variety on-line).
guardian.co.uk/media
Guardian Unlimited editor Emily Bell is always prescient and highly informed
about TV and New Media.
www.bbc.co.uk/writersroom
www.finaldraft.com
Writer's Guild Of America: www.wga.org
Writers Guild Of Great Britain: www.writersguild.org.uk

INDEX

143